Work's Intimacy

@Jason_a_w

Work's Intimacy

Melissa Gregg

polity

First published in 2011 by Polity Press
Reprinted 2011

Polity Press
65 Bridge Street
Cambridge CB2 1UR, UK

Polity Press
350 Main Street
Malden, MA 02148, USA

ISBN-13: 978-0-7456-5027-2
ISBN-13: 978-0-7456-5028-9 (pb)

A catalogue record for this book is available from the British Library.

Typeset in 10.5 on 12 pt Sabon
by Toppan Best-set Premedia Limited
Printed and bound in Great Britain by the MPG Books Group

The publisher has used its best endeavours to ensure that the URLs for external websites referred to in this book are correct and active at the time of going to press. However, the publisher has no responsibility for the websites and can make no guarantee that a site will remain live or that the content is or will remain appropriate.

Every effort has been made to trace all copyright holders, but if any have been inadvertently overlooked the publisher will be pleased to include any necessary credits in any subsequent reprint or edition.

For further information on Polity, visit our website: www.politybooks.com

Contents

List of Figures

Acknowledgments

A three-year Australian Research Council Postdoctoral Discovery Fellowship supported this research from 2007–9. Thanks to Graeme Turner for his help in the draft stages of the application and for so much more since. Further assistance for the project came from a University of Queensland Foundation Research Excellence Award in 2007. This grant helped to fund the team of research assistants that made this book possible: Neil Harvey, Ian Rogers, Nadia Mizner, Sarah Xu, and Bo McGrath. I am grateful to all of them.

Colleagues at the Centre for Critical and Cultural Studies at the University of Queensland and the Department of Gender and Cultural Studies at the University of Sydney have been wonderfully forgiving of my own work habits. I have made many close friends in the long hours spent in the Forgan Smith Tower and the Quadrangle, with and without the assistance of technology. On the domestic front, thanks to Rachel O'Reilly, Jason Wilson, and Catriona Menzies-Pike. Also to the many online friends who have kept us occupied in and out of each other's company.

For help with the manuscript, special thanks to Geert Lovink, Graeme Turner, Terry Flew, and Michelle Dicinoski. For invitations and support to present this material overseas, I particularly thank Rosalind Gill, Andy Pratt, Mark Banks, Stephanie Taylor, Adi Kuntsman, David Hesmondhalgh, Gavin Stewart, Alexis Wheedon, Greg Seigworth, and Trebor Scholz. For feedback, references, solidarity and provocation thanks to Lauren Berlant, Kris Cohen, Genevieve Bell, Mark Deuze, Jo Littler, Helen Kennedy, John Clarke,

Mark Andrejevic, Zala Volcic, Jack Qiu, James Hay, and Jack Bratich.

Anyone working in the field of cultural labor owes a great debt to Angela McRobbie and Andrew Ross. Their pioneering studies of work have been major inspirations for this project. I would also like to thank John Caldwell, Alan Liu, Barbara Ehrenreich, and Arlie Russell Hochschild for writing books that demonstrate the kind of analysis I would like to aspire to.

A publishing subsidy from the Australian Academy of the Humanities allowed images to be included in the book. Thanks to John Thompson for supporting this request and for the opportunity to publish with Polity. I am deeply grateful to the University of Sydney for the support to travel regularly in the last stages of this project and test the ideas to larger audiences.

My greatest thanks are to the participants who gave their precious time to provide material for this study. May your work and home lives continue to animate and secure the intimacies you most desire.

Preface

When I moved to Brisbane in early 2004, a number of Sydney friends made it clear I should expect few visitors. To Australia's southern residents, the large north-eastern state of Queensland remains a curiosity, summoning images of sun-drenched lethargy, backward attitudes, conservative farmers, and corrupt law enforcement. The state capital Brisbane has long been regarded by residents and outsiders alike as a "sleepy little town." Indeed, in the period this book describes, glossy tourism brochures began to use this phrase as a slogan, adding, "can you blame us?" in an attempt to celebrate the developing night-time economy. In spite of such prejudice, I was one of the thousands of interstate migrants who moved to the Sunshine State for a full-time job in the past decade. And even though substantial newspaper coverage and government rhetoric placed great hope in these statistics, the experiences of actual workers largely went missing from the public record. This book captures just a few of them.

This research is based on a three-year Australian Research Council Postdoctoral Fellowship from 2007–9. *Working From Home: New Media Technology, Workplace Culture and the Changing Nature of Domesticity* aimed to offer empirical evidence of technology's impact on the work and home lives of employees in the information and communication spheres of the knowledge economy. Large organizations were chosen – in education, government, broadcasting, and telecommunications – to contrast the many depictions of self-employed, entrepreneurial workers at the leading edge of the "new economy." From four employers, 26 participants were recruited at different levels of the workplace hierarchy. Employees were interviewed annually for the three-year period when this was possible. Their names have been anonymized for publication.

While constraints on time prevented extensive ethnographic engagement with workers, a number of wider social developments inform the reflections that follow. At the level of politics, a federal election with a strong emphasis on workers' rights saw the Australian Labor Party triumph in 2007 after 12 years in opposition. Within just a couple of months, the global economy endured a violent downward swing, which pushed Australia from prosperity to near recession, bringing unprecedented levels of national debt. Meanwhile the project's focus, communications technology, facilitated the tremendous uptake of social networking sites – from MySpace to Facebook, and a later surge to Twitter. In the final year of the study, the commercial release of the iPhone in Australia changed the telecommunications landscape significantly. The book now stands as an archive of this phenomenal rise of social media, and the growth of Internet use in everyday life.

In describing the lived impact of the new economy's "flexible" workplace, however, the project originates from an earlier downturn. The sustained glamorization of entrepreneurial business culture since the dot.com boom is the lasting legacy of a complex historical moment that few studies have interrogated sufficiently. Across any number of cultural artifacts today, computers and networked devices remain the resilient index of a variety of social changes, from family relations to commerce, even dating practices. But nothing has been more evident – and more absent from political discussion – than the way that online connectivity consummates the middle-class infatuation with work.

This book shows the extent to which new media technology encourages and exacerbates a much older tendency among salaried professionals to put work at the heart of daily concerns, often at the expense of all other sources of intimacy and fulfillment. The growing magnetism of mobile communication devices is one of the strongest indications that there is now a significant number of people for whom paid employment is the most compelling demonstration of virtue, accomplishment, and self-identity that society makes available. With a range of online subcultures also developing in support of these tendencies, the mutually reinforcing benefits of chronic connectivity among educated professionals are highly circular. At a time of declining civic participation, pressures on the institutions of marriage and the family, and persistent religious and racial intolerance in the West, this book offers a new lens for analytical attention. It explains how ordinary workers may withdraw from a range of more complex human relationships to focus on a proven source of personal esteem – their job – since its rewards are so openly celebrated in the dominant register for modern relationships: the capitalist marketplace.

All books are difficult to write, but this one has been especially affected by my own implication in the phenomena under discussion. Coming to terms with work's intimacy has entailed moving states and cities more than once in search of what may be an elusive fit between personal and professional motives. On a more troubling level, it has also meant learning alongside others the grammar of hunched shoulders, clandestine drinking cultures, RSI prevention, and enforced leave. This project has presented a complex scholarly dilemma, which is the difficulty of distinguishing among participants' revelations about work, the behavior of peers and colleagues, and my own lived practice. It concludes with a strong conviction that the present generation of academics must be among the first to see their lives and loves as potentially open to change.

Introduction: Work's Intimacy

Performing Professionalism
Online and On the Job

No-one's job is safe.

Australian Federal Industry Minister
Kim Carr, February 2009

This book provides an overdue account of online technology and its impact on work life. It moves between the offices and homes of today's salaried professionals to provide an intimate insight into the personal, family and wider social tensions faced by workers in a changing employment landscape. For any number of years now, new media technology has been marketed as giving us the freedom to work where we want, when we want, in flexible arrangements that apparently suit the conditions of the modern office. But little has been written to illustrate the consequences of this development, where work has broken out of the office, downstairs to the cafe, in to the street, on to the train, and later still to the living room, dining room, and bedroom.

Online technology has brought some significant problems to the work and personal lives of ordinary office workers – the information workers at the heart of the so-called "knowledge economy." This book describes the experiences of these employees, focusing on the information, communication and education ("ICE") professions that complement the heavy-hitting "FIRE" sectors of finance, insurance and real estate.[1] The latter have enjoyed their own chroniclers of late. The global economic downturn generated a predictable flurry of insider accounts of work cultures at the top end of town, as well as the housing and loan schemes that precipitated much of the wider disaster. *Work's Intimacy* provides a different white-collar story. It reflects the lives of those in much more mundane office environments, in a city with a significant case of suburban sprawl. But in a digitally connected "network society" (Castells 2000), these workers' livelihoods are no less affected in the shift from prosperity to recession – and back again.

The following chapters demonstrate the increasingly intimate relationship salaried professionals have with their work, and how new media technologies are involved in this development. Most obviously, online technology changes our sense of availability in professional information jobs. Communication platforms and devices allow work to invade spaces and times that were once less susceptible to its presence. This is a process we might describe the *presence bleed* of contemporary office culture, where firm boundaries between personal and professional identities no longer apply. Presence bleed explains the familiar experience whereby the location and time of work become secondary considerations faced with a "to do" list that seems forever out of control. It not only explains the sense of responsibility workers feel in making themselves ready and willing to work beyond paid hours, but also captures the feeling of anxiety that arises in jobs that involve a never-ending schedule of tasks that must be fulfilled – especially since there are not enough workers to carry the load. Throughout this book, workers will be shown to use online networks in the home to catch up on work that can't be finished in the office, as roles expand and employees are asked to do "more with less." With the increased use of digital technology, workloads that may have been acceptable to begin with are shown to accumulate further expectations and responsibilities that aren't being recognized – and never will be, if home-based work continues to go unremarked. Like the mobile devices facilitating this workload, the jobs themselves are subject to "function creep." The purported convenience of the technologies obscures the amount of additional work they demand. As one young librarian in this study explained: "They're not reducing any work load, they're just giving us more stuff to do. You kind of think something has to give, you know, you can't just keep piling work on us."

Presence bleed captures both the changing behavioral dimensions and professional expectations in communication- and information-heavy jobs. For the middle-class employees this condition affects, networked technologies are affordable enough to have in the home, so when online connections allow access to work beyond office hours, the possibility of being willing and able to work can manifest as a compulsion that has to be monitored.[2] To some extent, this is a result of the sense of fulfillment and gratification many workers derive from their job, which makes them susceptible to letting professional duties spill into other times and spaces. But for just as many, the coerciveness of online technology allows employers to contact them beyond paid hours as a matter of course, whether or not this is explicitly acknowledged. In either case, consciousness of the always-present potential for engaging with work is a new form of affective labor that must be constantly regulated.[3]

The professionals in this book engage in work beyond the formal work day for a range of reasons. For some, it's to "keep sane" amidst a constant tide of communication requests that a hectic schedule cannot accommodate. For others, it's to maintain perceptions of competence and professionalism surpassing the call of duty – to reassure clients of their importance, or to keep the rest of "the team" happy. In the absence of formal policies regarding new media use, particularly when it comes to email response times, the stories they tell reveal online devices to be part of an armory of psychological preparedness that workers bring to their jobs even before the workday begins. Online technology allows workers to carve out strategies to cope with conditions that are highly intensified because they are taken to be individual rather than structural in nature.

In some ways, this behavior accords with ideas of neoliberal governance in which workers take responsibility for their actions and enjoy this as a form of freedom (Rose 1999a, 1999b). "Working from home" can perhaps be read as a kind of personal and professional cohesiveness employees establish to make individualized working conditions palatable. Retreating from an office environment that appears to obstruct the completion of core job tasks, workers choose to conduct some of the most critical parts of their professional practice from home. For women in particular, this appears to be a way of coping with the lack of flexibility in the performance, attendance and reward measures that continue to guide the formal workplace. Subsequent chapters show women are prepared to wait until the cooking and cleaning are done, and the rest of the house is asleep, to have time alone to work. Having time alone with one's paid work can even become a form of solace from other, dubiously recognized, labors.

"I can't work at work" is also a common expression for employees introduced in this book who find the workplace full of unnecessary deviations. What's interesting is that the bulk of these "distractions" come in the form of interaction with other employees. One of the greatest benefits of online technology is therefore to moderate preferred levels of collegial engagement. Remoteness can be feigned in spite of physical presence, just as presence can be simulated when employees are actually out of the office. In either case, the coercive nature of "face-time" is one of the many "inefficiencies" of the office that play a role in driving employees home to work.

But as professional concerns claim a larger stake in the activities and priorities of the home, employees risk placing themselves in a position where employers will no longer feel obliged to provide effective compensation for their efforts. The lengthening workday can't be recognized in the spreadsheet formulae that calculate the hours served by modern employees. Moreover as economic conditions deteriorate – and employees are asked to accept reduced hours or pay cuts for the benefit of the company bottom line – an already large gulf between motivation, incentive and reward for salaried work comes in to play. The self-directed employee of the future may be less susceptible to the ties that bind their labor to an employer.[4]

The work/life ruse

In the years preceding the recent economic downturn, a range of commentators failed to appreciate the extent to which middle-class professionals had been encouraged to see work as the most significant demonstration of their success and identity. Feminists in particular seemed more interested in popular culture as a gauge for political accomplishments (or lack thereof) leaving workplace concerns to the dwindling ranks of union members and organizers.[5] While business was booming, men and women each worked long hours for firms that were more than happy to profit from their "sacrificial labor" (Ross 2004). The refusal to mount a sustained critique of long hours culture, and the gendered assumptions underpinning it, had the effect of making women feel grateful for so-called "flexible" work arrangements. These were conditions that allowed women to maintain traditional childcare and home maintenance expectations but only in addition to paid work (see chapter 2).

Sociologists, management literature and HR directives provided a powerful discourse encouraging employees to pursue "work–life balance" as a necessary corrective to the high performance demands of entrenched work cultures. That this trend coincided with an increased number of women in the workplace only served to imply such balance was their particular concern. It couldn't admit that work in itself might not be the problem; that many people enjoy their job for the sense of accomplishment it can bring. Nor could it appreciate that leaders of organizations play a key role in generating, facilitating and maintaining workloads. The language of work–life balance in fact absolved management for the human resourcing decisions defining their employees' experience. Little wonder that it was taken up with such fervor in workplace training initiatives and a raft of complimentary "coping with stress", "dealing with change" and "time management" workshops. These well-funded measures were the ideological ruse disguising the concrete calculations being made to affect the bulk of employees' workloads. Their effect was to imply that individuals who could not cope with growing job requirements were at personal fault.

As a solution to workplace ills, "work–life balance" also ignored another momentous point. Well-off employees who gain pleasure from their work aren't likely to want to balance it with other things. Leisure pursuits or personal relationships may prove more difficult, costly, emotionally complicated, and altogether less satisfying for a range of personalities. As Arlie Hochschild (1997) has demonstrated, the work world offers a range of consolations when one's private life may demand more effort and less reward than the clearly defined, routine satisfactions of paid pursuits. Today's workplaces can be infinitely attractive to women who may not know how to improve the household division of labor without risking their marriage, but who can rely on legislation to ensure equity in the office (which she doesn't also have to clean). For middle-class women, equal opportunity in the public arena may have revealed how very few home-based pleasures can compete with the interest and excitement to be found in paid work.[6] The notion of "work–life balance" is inadequate "not only because it seems to arrive when women enter full-time employment" – which downplays the gender norms that were central to the Fordist economy (see also Pateman 1988; Mitropoulos 2006) – it also assumes "a classic (Marxian) understanding of work as alienating" (Adkins and Jokinen 2008: 144). But "only alienating work needs to be balanced out or mitigated against by home, family, and leisure time" (ibid.). In a cultural context that regularly celebrates the status and rewards of creative work – indeed, as new media jobs purposefully collapse the boundaries between work and play – a new vocabulary is needed.[7]

This book provides evidence to suggest that professional work generates forms of pleasure and accomplishment that rival the markers of identity favored in previous historical formations. This is what online technology and its growing list of applications finally allows us to see. These pleasures and intimacies underwrite professional workers' willingness to engage in work outside paid hours, just as they provide justification for abandoning other forms of experience and fulfillment that stand in their way. The most successful online platforms of recent years, social networking sites, build on the deliberate confusion of work and friendship that have been hallmarks of professional middle-class office cultures for decades. The hegemony of the "contact" in office software packages worldwide promotes this deliberately blurry line between professional and personal etiquette. And in spite of numerous efforts to claim these developments as positive, onerous terms of service and obscure privacy settings of web platforms like Facebook showed the profits to be made from making bourgeois business culture the new normal.

If the language of intimacy helps to demonstrate work's enticing and seductive dimensions, including the social dimensions to work that will be elaborated in later chapters, it also forces recognition of the ease with which these aspects have been aligned with capitalist profits. Online culture's incredible capacity to quantify and instrumentalize friendship is one of the main trends this book highlights. Appreciating work's intimacy in this sense helps to pinpoint what is at stake in the move to work-centered identities and cultures. That is, if our capacities for intimacy are most regularly exercised in the pursuit of competitive professional profit, we face the prospect of being unable to appreciate the benefits of intimacy for unprofitable purposes. The consequences this poses for society are of course troubling, and so a backwards glance in time may help establish the extent to which this trend should cause us alarm.

A history of networking

The email-equipped mobile phone and wireless laptop are just the latest in a range of always-on devices offering ample opportunity for work to follow us out of the office. They pose new questions for the notion of professionalism as the workday adjusts to fit new surroundings. Should I answer that email tonight after my last glass of wine? Do I have to be friends with my colleagues on Facebook? Will my son know if I'm listening to him from the other room as I finish this overdue presentation? Does my boss even know when I am at work?

But just how different are these dilemmas from previous manifestations of office life? In the drive to understand the novelty of online culture, few have noted the links between social networking practices of the present and those of white-collar work in previous decades.[8] This has had the knock-on effect of missing what may be unique about the cultures of online communities, as Part II of this book elaborates. In 1936, a modest self-help volume began to attract the attention of business readers seeking advice to navigate matters of etiquette and manners in professional contexts. Originally published to bring together a series of lectures by its author, Dale Carnegie, *How to Win Friends and Influence People* described a range of skills useful for life and business. The tips imparted in the book included how to deliver a compliment, how to appear friendly and genuine to colleagues, and how to apologize convincingly – all of which would help to ensure ongoing collegiality in the workplace. Carnegie's anecdotal approach may sound quaint to today's readers, but with sales of over 15 million, its effects have been lasting. This manual of pleasantries not only offers an important archive of white male business culture (particularly in its earlier editions); it also marks the beginning of an entire industry for what we might call *management* self-help.[9] Carnegie's book is a relic of a time when women were a rarity in the office, men survived on reputation and a job was ostensibly for life. As the television series *Mad Men* also illustrates, in this white-collar world, a businessman's main priority was to cultivate a reliable and likable personality that could be traded for a certain level of security. Before Human Resources policies and modulated induction training, *How to Win Friends and Influence People* was part of a soon to be flourishing genre of business manuals that helped workers identify appropriate behavior for the workplace. This was a time when the very idea of professionalism for the growing middle classes had yet to take hold (cf. Liu 2004: chapter 2). Carnegie's classic provides an early precedent for understanding the deliberate confusion of friendship and business interests that are ongoing concerns of this book.

A number of authors in the years since, among them William H. Whyte (1963/1956) and C. Wright Mills (1951), advanced sociological understandings of the white-collar mindset. Whyte's "organization man" of the 1950s, for instance, was a diligent, mobile employee who could expect to move through a succession of "company towns" in tandem with his elevation up the career ladder. The mutual bond captured in the title of Whyte's book was as much a description of the kinds of loyalty expected between employer and worker as it was an indictment of mindless corporate ambition. In fact, Whyte's writing still speaks of a time when one could believe that a "social ethic" could be pursued through affiliation with an outstanding business. The worker could depend on a return on his investment in the company so long as the latter maintained a convincing vocational narrative and enviable position within the community. Whyte distinguished between the "well-rounded man" of the organization, who is successful, but not *too* successful (1963: 125), and "the executive," whom he endearingly terms the "not-well-rounded man." The well-rounded worker followed the principle: "be loyal to the company and the company will be loyal to you," and he had particular insights to share:

> On the matter of overwork they are particularly stern. They want to work hard, but not too hard; the good, equable life is paramount and they see no conflict between enjoying it and getting ahead. The usual top executive, they believe, works much too hard, and there are few subjects upon which they will discourse more emphatically than the folly of elders who have a single-minded devotion to work.

Whyte further observes:

> Out of necessity, then, as well as natural desire, the wise young man is going to enjoy himself – plenty of time with the kids, some good hobbies . . . obtrusive in no particular, excessive in no zeal. He will be the man in the middle. (1963: 127)

The executive, by contrast, is described in part three of Whyte's book, which has the telling title: "The Neuroses of Organization Man."

> Common to these men is an average work week that runs between 50 and 60 hours. Typically, it would break down something like this: each weekday the executive will put in about 9 1/2 hours in the office. Four out of five weekdays he will work nights. One night he will be booked for business entertaining, another night he will probably spend at the office or in a protracted conference somewhere else.

> On two of the other nights he goes home. But it's no sanctuary he retreats to; it's a branch office. While only a few go so far as to have a room equipped with dictating machines, calculators, and other appurtenances of their real life, most executives make a regular practice of doing the bulk of their business reading at home and some find it the best time to do their most serious business phone work ("I do a lot of spot-checking by phone from home," one executive explained. "I have more time then, and besides most people have their guard down when you phone them at home.")

Whyte's description predates the BlackBerry by, say, 50 years, but it is a fascinating portent of today's office cultures: "In one company, the top executives have set up a pool of Dictaphones to service executives who want to take them home, the better to do more night and weekend work. In almost all companies the five-day week is pure fiction."

These details allow us to appreciate that technology has long facilitated particular work styles and preferences, especially for a business demographic. But Whyte goes on to examine the rationale that is offered for engaging in this work-focused lifestyle. "In talking about why he works," Whyte surmises: "the executive does not speak first of service, or of pressures from the organization; very rarely does he mention his family as a reason. He speaks of himself – and the demon within him. He works because his ego demands it." For these personalities, work is the dominant focus. And even though their wives, doctors and friends all warn them that they work too hard, the executive maintains that outside parties "didn't understand" (1963: 139). These words are worth remembering in the course of this book, since they echo the language used by many study participants to explain their reasons for working at home. As new technologies make the possibility of connecting to work an effortless proposition, it is not just the leaders and managers of organizations that are driven to work. Ordinary workers and the most junior employees show the habits and dispositions of Whyte's executives. In the terms of his analysis, a growing number of employees in today's workplaces are "not-well-rounded."

Of the two writers, C. Wright Mills is perhaps the more critical. *White Collar* provides a more extensive historical description of the changes in occupation and demography in the move from rural to urban life in the United States. In doing so, Mills conveys a sense of foreboding about the emergence of the professional class in the 1950s and its particular obsessions. From the feudal communities of one era to the autonomous secularism taking hold, Mills anticipated that individuals would face growing difficulties in their working relationships in future. "In the movement from authority to manipulation," he warned, "power shifts from the visible to the invisible, from the known to the anonymous. And with rising material standards, exploitation becomes less material and more psychological" (Mills 1951: 110). Alan Liu develops these observations in *The Laws of Cool: Knowledge Work and the Culture of Information* (2004). In a wide-ranging book, one of the first to extensively theorize the impact of online culture on corporate practice, Liu suggests that to gauge "the tone of modern emotional experience" we must look not to the sphere of private life but to "the great impersonal organizations of modernity – above all, the workplace" (2004: 89). Like Mills, Liu sees that the key feature

distinguishing the move to urban-based office work is in the appropriate regulation of affect:

> However important it was for a child to learn to manage anger in
> the presence of father or mother, it was now even more important
> that father and mother learn to manager their anger, resentment, joy,
> lust, distraction, or boredom in a workplace cut off from the farm
> or town that had been the customary, ambient field of emotion.
> (2004: 90)

In Liu's account, the office embodies the dominant protocols for
the manners, skills and relationships necessary to succeed in modern
life, something Carnegie's book also foretold. Here we can note how
practices like online social networking extend the scope for today's
workers seeking to acquire the skills necessary for professional
success. Liu's updated reading of workplace culture displays frank
abandonment of any lingering expectation of meritocracy or security as factors in the rise up the company hierarchy. Written at a
time when mass layoffs had become commonplace in white-collar
work, Liu explains that to be a "professional-managerial-technical
worker now is to stake one's authority on an even more precarious
knowledge that has to be re-earned with every new technological
change, business cycle, or downsizing in one's own life" (2004: 19).
Instead of the linear career path described by earlier writers, this
experience constitutes "the foundationless suspense, the perpetual
anxiety" of knowledge work which involves a combination of self-
auditing, life-long learning, and the successful performance of corporate "cool" (ibid.).

Liu's idea of "professional cool" draws on a history of feminist
scholarship establishing the significance of "emotion work" in a
range of occupations. In the United States, Arlie Russell Hochschild
(1983) pioneered efforts to demonstrate the "affective" labor in
service industry jobs, which can be physically tiring in the same way
as apparently more physical, "manual" work. Hochschild's early
research studying airline hostesses and parking infringement officers
showed the traumatic impact of working with the general public in
emotionally volatile situations. Employees risk their own psychological health in their efforts to manipulate the emotions of others and
simultaneously perform "service with a smile." Workers therefore
become accustomed to "deep acting" so that the needs of the job and
their own desires ultimately become aligned. Hochschild provided
important empirical insight into the forms of psychological exploitation that Mills anticipated would be felt in a growing number of jobs.

The flexible work persona of office life today is a further development from these studies. While the service worker seeks to control outwardly directed emotions for business profit, the knowledge worker's affective labor operates in the opposite direction. It is devoted to developing reserves of emotional resilience to withstand the ontological challenges of the typical workday. Later chapters show the extent of employees' investment in work and their subsequent exhaustion – whether from immediate job demands in poorly resourced offices or from the perpetual anxiety of not knowing what is to be expected in any given day. Liu captures this new landscape for work in his description of "the damned middle managers, who when laid off in the millions are by and large irrevocably shunted off the track of traditional job security and career growth into a wholly different school of hard knocks" (2004: 45). This is a fate of "purely lateral career movement, permanent re- or deskilling, and long-term salary and benefits reduction" (ibid.). While these words were written in the fallout from the economic context of the 1990s, the picture of mid-career instability reflects the fate of a number of workers in this book. A significant number of participants encountered redundancy, retraining, job changes or relocation during the course of our meetings. Of those still employed by the same organizations, several were unsure of their ongoing prospects. Work was regularly redesigned and assigned to dwindling ranks of employees, albeit in a language and on terms intended to make this feel empowering. An early promotion is not empowering if it makes your workload paralyzing, but with few staff members ever available to shoulder the incessant expectations of information jobs, a lack of training and time is now to be expected – another consequence of management parsimony.

An absence of long-term organizational strategy affects workers' capacity to predict their workload or ask for existing benefits as previous forms of responsibility and entitlement are turned on their head. These are workplaces composed of "multi-competent work teams" who "oversee projects holistically with perspective on total company strategy" (Liu 2004: 46). This is what we hear from project officers who color-code their email according to required response times to juggle a host of ongoing jobs with multiple stakeholders and hierarchies. It is in the comments of the junior PR strategist who regularly covers for a boss too busy to answer her own email. It is in the foresight of the expectant mother who subscribes to home broadband so that she can continue to run her department while on maternity leave. The function creep affecting workers' roles comes from a lack of specificity regarding the limits of job descriptions that cannot keep pace with an accelerated workplace. And all along the acceleration of workloads is heightened by the processing capacities and ubiquitous availability encouraged by communications technology.

Emotional labor

Liu's writing is also useful for noting the particular combination of affect regulation and emotional distance required of workers dependent on communications technology for daily interaction. As computers entered the workplace, "It was not one's boss or manager that forbade laughing, weeping, cursing, shouting, or celebrating" on the job. Rather, "it was a blank cubicle wall that simply shut off social interaction and, within that cubicle, database forms that accepted not a jot of humor, not a single expletive" (Liu 2004: 118). In this grim view, software packages and poor office design each contribute to a dehumanized workplace by preventing social relations with colleagues. The present book extends this analysis to the post-dot. com juncture, where open-plan offices break down space barriers but pose new problems of collegial over-exposure and enforced intimacy. Meanwhile online platforms provide the potential for *endless* outpourings of emotion and spontaneity, delivering precisely those affective pleasures Liu worries have been lost from the professional workplace. Twitter tweets and status updates offer regular breaks from the dull patter of solitary typing, though it remains to be seen how long these subcultures of support will withstand the surveillance proclivities of employers. As chapters 5 and 6 explain, there is no easy distinction between the blank corporate space of the office and the codified intimacy of Facebook, especially as more and more organizations seek to utilize social networking sites for profit.

Liu argues that there is "no recreational outside" (2004: 77) to knowledge work – any resistance typically takes place within the same confines of the cubicle and the computer screen (Gregg 2009a). For both women and men, the workplace has become a "vast, compelling, dramatic, socially shared world" compared to the lifeless suburban neighborhoods they leave behind each day (Hochschild, in Wilson and Lande 2005: 276). This book documents a period when management techniques responded to the desires of workers at all levels to exercise autonomy, giving rise to the feelings of enterprise and esteem central to work's psychological appeal. As Luc Boltanski and Eve Chiapello argue, the "new spirit of capitalism" revolutionizes past models of employment because it "guarantees the workers' commitment without recourse to compulsion, by making everyone's work meaningful" (2005: 76). The fulfilling nature of contemporary jobs, at least at the level of institutional rhetoric, rewards employees for being self-motivated agents, ready and willing to work: "everyone knows what they must do without having to be told. Firm direction is given without resorting to orders, and employees can continue to organize themselves. Nothing is imposed on them since they subscribe to the project" (ibid.).

Like Liu, Boltanski and Chiapello show how appropriate affect is the route to employee complicity with these new demands of the workplace. Workers can be relied upon "to control themselves, which involves transferring constraints from external organizational mechanisms to people's internal dispositions" (2005: 79). Those with ongoing positions in today's workplaces face a constant stream of requests to assess their own productivity in compliance with efficiency targets. Self-monitoring and individual goal-setting become disciplinary techniques by which employees engage in the "deep acting" required to implement management tenets. The autonomy of salaried work comes at a price: to constantly prove responsibility.

Intimate work

With this overview, we have some sense of what has changed about office culture in recent decades. First of all, if salaried jobs have always relied on networking skills for reputation management and career progression, increasingly there are fewer material and psychological rewards for engaging in these practices. In fact, as subsequent chapters testify, job security is no longer attained as a consequence of social networking. Rather, networking is an additional form of labor that is required to demonstrate ongoing employability. The crucial difference is that the stability of a permanent job is no longer an end result of the practice. The practice is itself the job; the only thing assumed is that any hallmarks of security will remain elusive. As Boltanski and Chiapello explain, the "activity par excellence" for workers in information jobs "is integrating oneself into networks." To network is "to put an end to isolation, and have opportunities for meeting people or associating with things, proximity to which is liable to generate a project" (2005: 110). In information jobs, the content of the project is less important than the general fact of activity. The priority is for employees "never to be short of a project, bereft of an idea, always to have something in mind, in the pipeline, with other people one meets out of a desire to do something" (ibid.).[10]

In this book, workers without something "in the pipeline" were the first to suffer during the downturn. But those who survived also suffered costs in the quest to maintain multiple "projects." By making a virtue of individuals' capacities to juggle competing commitments at once, employers avoided the responsibility of providing adequate support and reassurance for workers. Legitimate feelings of instability and overload were dealt with by "professional development courses" designed to ease the anxiety arising from constant churn. They were later met with requests to accept reduced hours or extended unpaid leave. Such gestures placed the onus on employees to develop the emotional and psychological capacity to withstand positions and workloads with no definitive beginning or end. Paolo Virno notes the consequences of this "dramatic lack of foundation" in the workplace:

> Fears of particular dangers, if only virtual ones, haunt the workday like a mood that cannot be escaped. This fear, however, is transformed into an operational requirement, a special tool of the trade. Insecurity about one's place during periodic innovation, fear of losing recently gained privileges, and anxiety about being "left behind" translate into flexibility, adaptability, and a readiness to reconfigure oneself. (1996: 17)

Communication technologies play a key role in these broader shifts. The surveillance capabilities of many online applications create new dilemmas as social networking sites, calendar scheduling devices, chat programs and above all email bring a raft of opportunities and requirements for work-related contact. Future chapters illustrate in detail how workers retain a sense of privacy in this transformed professional realm, and what strategies are useful to survive a networked office with its never-ending flow of information and communication demands. The process of professional reconfiguration is underway at pace.

Labor politics has always rested on the notion that limits must be placed on the workday. In an era of presence bleed, the possibility of asserting absence from the workplace becomes a matter of intense concern. If the office exists in your phone, how is it possible to claim the right to be away from it for any length of time? Indeed, how do employees assert the right to avoid work-related contact if the bulk of their colleagues are friends? Labor activism is powerless to meet these challenges with its current vocabulary. Like never before, communications technologies grant access to the workplace beyond

physical constraints, just as workplace intimacies trouble the sense
of what is coerced or freely chosen labor. To give a sense of the
stories to follow, note how policy officer Jenny combines notions of
professional performance, diligence and anxiety in explaining her
approach to answering email:

> I feel that if I don't answer an email someone thinks I'm purposely
> ignoring them instead of I haven't read it yet . . . It's a concern and
> it's also just how I see myself as a professional. I want people to know
> I am looking after things, and I think sometimes when you send an
> email out, if you don't get anything back, you don't know whether
> they're ignoring it, dealing with it, thinking about it, pending a
> response – and I want people to know that if they send an email to
> me, I'm actioning it.

A defining feature of Jenny's sense of professionalism is her
approach to email monitoring. As other responses in the study will
show, a platform that was first designed to overcome the asynchro-
nous schedules of co-workers has been transformed into its opposite.
It is now a means to demonstrate co-presence with colleagues and
enhance the pace and immediacy of busy office schedules. The complicity between always-on technologies and emerging forms of
workplace subjectivity are powerful disciplinary incitements for
Jenny to engage in what might otherwise appear as compulsive
behavior. For she admits: "I think that the anxiety I have with emails
is absolutely ridiculous. I just think it's stupid; I should get over it.
I don't think it's something that's placed upon me; I think it's truly
a personal manifestation."

Whether a personal choice, an addiction or simply a sensible
response to new norms in the workplace, Jenny is one of many
workers trapped in some very unhealthy habits. While her comments
are evidence of her commitment to her job, they also indicate that
her workload is a transaction and a performance that must be
managed alone. She is apologetic about her ability to adequately
cope with her email, as if it is an individual failing. She doesn't see
that her experience is shared across professions and industries, that
it is the result of widespread policy failure, and that ultimately these
problems can be addressed.

Ordinary offices

In contrast to accounts of the new economy that take their cues from
Silicon Valley or Wall Street, it is important that this book is set in
a bunch of unremarkable office blocks amidst the traffic snarl of

boom-time Brisbane. It depicts a far from glamorous yet highly familiar reality encapsulated in the image of a grey workstation dominated by a recent model Dell desktop computer running Microsoft Outlook. It is a vision of technology so ordinary as to be mundane – and yet it is a vision that so many "new media" scholars seem resolutely prepared to ignore. The uptake of communications devices in mainstream jobs has brought a conclusive end to utopian dreams that the Internet will revolutionize the working day. While there have been changes to the average nine-to-five job, this book shows that these are minimal at best. The power of entrenched business interests is no more evident than in the speed with which online technology moved from offering hope for a better workplace to becoming one of the most onerous dimensions of work life today – often in the very language of freedom.

Anyone who has spent cocktail hour in the airline lounge of a capital city airport knows that the frequent flyer is the archetype for the new world of mobile work. Each weekday a stream of heavy hitting machos can be seen issuing orders through freshly minted BlackBerrys while enjoying complimentary house beverages and cable TV. For the majority of workers back at the office, the ones

Figure 0.1   Open-plan newsroom, Brisbane, 2007

Figure 0.2   Arts festival workstation; Outlook running on Dell

on the other end of the phone actioning these directives, the work-place is rather different. It is typically a static, banal and routine experience, in which emails and phone calls pile up throughout the day regardless of location or schedule. For these ordinary workers, technology adds another layer of work on top of what is already expected. And due to the hierarchies that persist in the majority of workplaces, the opportunities for escape are few.

This is the salaried class of office workers living in the suburbs of all kinds of cities who know the precise number of minutes it takes to commute to work. These are people for whom work is hardly "better than sex" (Trinca and Fox 2004) but who might feel a sense of recognition watching the BBC comedy *The Office*. Like the characters in Gervais's mockumentary, these workers need to believe that collegial pleasures and intimacies can be carved out of even the most hopeless management cultures. They may or may not lament the lessening distinction between their personal and profes-sional identities, but if this study is any indication, they feel quite powerless to stop the structural influences forcing this change upon them in the name of flexibility and efficiency.

For over a decade, online technologies have acted as orienting devices for the experience of career mobility negotiated by growing numbers of educated workers. As we'll see, these platforms provide opportunities for connection, community, and solidarity, generating relationships that complicate what we mean by the notion of "friendship." At the same time however, technology has played on feelings of instability, threat, and fear among workers facing an unstable employment landscape and the death of the linear career path. The worst of this behavior involves manic email monitoring, online presence performance, and the tyranny of the mobile phone among senior executives and junior on-call workers alike. These developments are symptomatic of a situation in which the assumed benefits of white-collar work in the past century – security and predictability – have perhaps finally been lost (Berlant 2008). The emotional tenor of the modern office is one in which middle-class professionals are asked to adjust to changing forms of privilege and entitlement – and to do so quickly, without complaint, in order to survive. Only recently, this has grown to include accepting the shock of unsustainable credit debts, the loss of long-term investments and cutbacks to paid work hours.

We have come a long way from the professional world of the "organization man," although some things remain familiar. Boltanski and Chiapello put a contemporary spin on C. Wright Mills's famous definition of the white-collar worker as one who enjoyed "no firm roots, no sure loyalties to sustain his life and give it a centre." Mills wondered: "perhaps because he does not know where he is going, he is in a frantic hurry; perhaps because he does not know what frightens him, he is paralysed with fear" (1951: xvi). Indeed, in spite of the relative privilege of salaried work, the persistent themes in accounts of office life are the affects of fear and anxiety. This ontological bearing so characteristic of white-collar work takes on new dimensions in an age of maximum flexibility (Ross 2009; Gill and Pratt 2008).

The professionals described in this book – those who have survived the redundancies already inflicted – look set to continue the strategies they have assembled to cope with working conditions that have been difficult for some time. By sharing their stories, I hope to begin a longer conversation about the better workplaces we might imagine for the future. Recognizing the value of a job in and of itself in the present climate has the potential effect of suspending efforts to resist workloads that have been so accelerated by new technology that they escape even the most steadfast efforts to manage them. In

Figure 0.3 Brisbane suburbia

providing a language to articulate the consequences of this new phenomenon, *Work's Intimacy* intends to be an indictment, if not also an elegy to the experience of "presence bleed." It should not need to be added that it is written with a sense of wonder at the consequences should even the wealthiest of nations fail to learn the lesson of valuing its workers.

Part I

The Connectivity Imperative:
Business Responses
to New Media

1

Selling the Flexible Workplace

The Creative Economy and New Media Fetishism

The lifestyle city

As the Australian summer drew to a close in March 2009 it was becoming possible to think that Queensland had finally shrugged the perceptions of provincialism that had been its historical destiny. This was the month that Anna Bligh became the first female in history to be elected Premier of an Australian state, just six months after another woman from Queensland, Quentin Bryce, was sworn in as the nation's first female Governor General. A year earlier, a Queenslander was elected to the office of Prime Minister and he appointed an old schoolmate Federal Treasurer. For a region often lampooned for its backward image and lack of relevance to the rest of the country, something significant was brewing in the North.

Beyond political markers, by 2009 the Queensland Government's "Smart State" policy, a platform designed to invest large sums of money to enhance the cultural and intellectual infrastructure of its capital, Brisbane, had also proven their purpose. A major renovation of the State Library and the construction of a new Gallery of Modern Art (GOMA) – both facing the picturesque river stretching through the center of the city – were the centerpiece of a newly revitalized arts and information precinct. The installation of a revolving tourist "eye," in the vein of London's signature riverside attraction, seemed to confirm the transformation of Brisbane's South Bank from its original function as World Expo site in 1988 to a national forum for cutting-edge arts and culture.

To this point, Brisbane had marketed itself as "the lifestyle city." Long-serving Labor Party Premier Peter Beattie (1998–2007) had seized every opportunity to brand his home town as part of the beaming, folksy image he projected to the media and interstate investors. By the middle of the decade, the slogan had been replaced with a "creative city" tag.[1] The transformations taking place in Brisbane seemed to confirm the lucrative profits of these concerted exercises in spin. A new "Green Bridge" stretching across the river south of the CBD had cut commuter traffic across major arterials, with a growing number of cycle paths and walking routes taking advantage of Brisbane's subtropical climate. Heading north, real estate developments around Breakfast Creek and Bowen Hills were bordered by bunting. Vast tracts of newly released commercial land promised to deliver a cosmopolitan playground for local office workers, complete with cocktail bars and boutique cinemas by the water. A new Mayor, Liberal Party candidate Campbell Newman, embarked on an ambitious system of underground tunnels to ease transport congestion. Meanwhile, plans for a footbridge linking north and south of the CBD were a striking testimony to the city's onward advance.

The combined impact of this major construction program tested the patience of long-time residents, already concerned at the influx of migrants to the city. In response, the local council launched a strategic billboard campaign to soothe citizen anxieties. "Living in Brisbane 2026" was a policy affirmation of the optimism required for the city's future, particularly since a history of political corruption had severely damaged its sense of pride in the past.[2] Brisbane Marketing Chief John Aitken explained: "We want to be a clean, green, and sustainable city. We're looking globally at where our future lies." But newspaper articles covering this transformation were quick to note that "for a city that still prides itself on cockroach races on Australia Day, Brisbane's road to Damascus experience may still be a work in progress."[3]

Of all these developments, one of the most notable was the opening of the Creative Industries Precinct at the Kelvin Grove campus of the Queensland University of Technology. Offering an array of training and study opportunities for locals who might imagine working in the very cultural sectors that policymakers now sought to promote, the CI complex remains a striking manifestation of government investment priorities of the period. To build the campus, a whole suburb was transformed from a mix of residential housing and disused army land to performance theaters, lecture space, and fashion studios. A social inclusion agenda also ensured housing commission beneficiaries mixed with students in the delis, cafes, and supermarkets constituting a new "urban village" (Klaebe 2006). Holding his trophy for Most Outstanding Actor at Australia's annual television awards in May 2009, *Underbelly* star Gyton Grantley made a point of thanking QUT for the training vital to his success. In one small gesture, the creative industries brand had taken center stage, and QUT's contribution to national culture was hard to ignore. With southern states facing major fallout from the financial crisis, Brisbane had become a genuine contender to rival Sydney and Melbourne as Australia's ideal creative city.

A year later, the picture had vastly changed. Premier Bligh's authority had all but vanished following a plan to sell off key state-owned assets in an effort to remain solvent amidst the financial crisis. Major construction projects and real estate developments in and around the CBD were suspended pending ongoing investment support. The business press lamented the declining number of cranes on Brisbane's skyline, a colloquial signifier of industry downturn. The Brisbane boom was brief and potent. Its effects barely had a chance to reach the many workers who moved cities during the decade in anticipation of its spoils.[4] In the rush to embrace the benefits of the new knowledge economy, this chapter shares lessons from a period when hopes for a better future were pitched on instrumental exercises in city branding. This is because, far from being a peripheral experience of work life in the knowledge economy, Brisbane remains a template for initiatives in creative cities policy development taking place on a global scale. The success of its creative industries education strategy continues to influence the study and career options of local and international students alike, just as the research arm of the QUT CI precinct – home of the larger, multi-stakeholder ARC Centre for Creativity and Innovation – plays a key role in shaping international debate (e.g., Flew and Cunningham 2010; Keane 2007). Beyond the boosterism of boardroom discourse, this chapter sheds light on the human effects of one city's changing economic fortunes, to set the scene for the more intimate stories that follow in the rest of the book.

The Smart State

A unique convergence of financial, academic, and political interests contributed to Brisbane's branding as the "Smart State."[5] Building on the transformation of Queensland's Gold Coast into a home for film and television production outsourced from the US (Ward and

O'Regan, 2007), Brisbane's status as creative city is one of the clearest examples available of state-sanctioned investment in cultural labor. This local venture is, however, part of a larger story unfolding in the wake of Richard Florida's *The Rise of the Creative Class* (2002) and its warm reception in policymaking circles. The message many distilled from Florida's book was that artistic and symbolic workers were a proven tonic to enhance quality of life, levels of tolerance, and cultural diversity in urban areas.

Cities across the globe have since engaged a range of efforts to design areas compelling enough to attract these talented – and typically wealthy – workers (Oakley 2004). A suite of criticisms that emerged against Florida's theory and methods (e.g., Lovink and Rossiter 2007; Banks 2009) failed to dampen the enthusiasm of politicians and business investors seeking solutions to the urban decay and social anomie attending the shift to post-industrial economies. Creative industries policies were central to the revitalization of UK cities under the broader "Cool Britannia" framework, and the model continues to offer compelling visions of economic prosperity in cultures and countries with greatly different administrative arrangements (Pratt 2009; Potts and Cunningham 2008).

For Brisbane in particular, the Smart State strategy and creative industries policy direction were opportunities to reimagine the city in the wake of the repressive regime of former Premier Joh Bjelke-Petersen. Throughout the 1970s, Queensland's unique system of political representation had allowed a powerful bloc of country voters to exert disproportionate influence on elections and maintain the conservative National Party in power. With only a single House of Parliament and hence few structures for legislative scrutiny, the government had been able to pursue a campaign of surveillance and intimidation against young people in the city, targeting activists and artists especially. Specific laws allowed police to disperse social gatherings without cause, which made protests of any kind illegal, and had the latent effect of preventing the development of independent music and cultural events. Notorious moonlight patrols ramped up the already heavy-handed policing of alternative lifestyles and modes of dress in daylight hours (Morrison 2007; Stafford 2006).

Against this backdrop, Brisbane needed a major exercise in rebranding to overcome perceptions that had been memorialized by Unkle Fats and the Parameters in the punk anthem: "Pig City."[6] The many residents who had left the state in fear during previous decades needed reassurance that they could return to a safe and supportive home town, just as interstate migrants needed strong evidence that the city's attitudes had changed. In this sense, Brisbane fits Andrew Ross's observation that "an element of desperation" accompanies the creative industries trend in cities seeking a competitive advantage in globalized markets (2008: 33). On the surface, such policies seem designed to cater for workers at the heart of the economy being promoted. In effect, however, sustainable work models are less of a focus for attention than the boosts to real estate value in boutique areas flourishing near creative "hubs." In Brisbane's flagship newspaper, *The Courier-Mail*, feature stories at the time contributed to the prospect of an economic boom by touting the city's affordances as a "head office heaven."[7] These PR pieces appearing in business and employment lift-outs highlighted the desirable rates for commercial space in comparison with other cities, as tax incentives from the state government attempted to woo firms from elsewhere.[8] Since their audience was generally local, such features played a key role in maintaining morale for those business owners and CEOs who had already made the decision to "head north." Yet their interests were clearly pitched around the company bottom line. The workers employed in the burgeoning knowledge and service economy were of comparably little concern.

Figure 1.1 Selling the Brisbane Boom: a cover page from the *Courier Mail*'s weekly careers lift-out halfway through the study; Within a few months the financial crisis was threatening hundreds of jobs © Newspix / Kevin Bull

The Brisbane boom

Brisbane's changing demographics were soon evident in the growing number of luxury apartments taking position along the waterfront. In inner-city suburbs like New Farm, old boarding hostels and iconic "Queenslander" ranch houses were sold off in their dozens for more profitable multi-occupier arrangements. An old electricity substation adjacent to the transformed Powerhouse Centre for Performing Arts – itself a redeployment of an actual power-generator plant from an earlier industrial era – was just one of many high-end property redevelopments conceived and completed in the years of this study. With its sweeping riverfront park and fortnightly Farmers' Market, New Farm was an optimal location both for Baby Boomers seeking a lifestyle change and youngsters from more expensive cities harboring hopes of a waterside address. In the nearby enclave of Teneriffe, exclusive homeware stores opened to cater for the surfeit of loft-style apartments available in disused shipping warehouses. This classic post-industrial gentrification process capitalized on decommissioned freight districts in picturesque areas, turning the workplaces of an old economy into the domestic leisure space of the new. Extra bus services were needed to service the influx of residents commuting to the city for work, while online start-ups, media broadcasters, design and fashion businesses offered more conveniently located employment for the city's nouveau riche. A steady rise in cafes and bars fueled the consumption habits of this cash-rich but time-poor professional clientele.

The jewel in the crown of Brisbane's transformation from "sleepy little town" to "funky urban district" was the makeover of Fortitude Valley.[9] Once a late-night haven for queers, punks, and misfits (not to mention the corrupt cops of the city's recent past), collaborations between the local city council and Creative Industries researchers provided economic modeling and research data to demonstrate the area's viability of as a "Special Entertainment Precinct" (Flew et al. 2001). Fortitude Valley was the first nightclub zone in the country to be accorded this status in July 2006. Existing residents protesting the development were met with well-funded billboard campaigns emphasizing the district's new slogan: "Loud and Proud." A host of measures, including special street signs, speed restrictions, and police patrols, took effect in designated late-night party hours. A substantial public relations exercise in local news media also ensured that parents of the thousands of outer-suburban revelers descending on the area each weekend felt assured of their safety and protection.[10]

The cover of *The Weekend Australian Magazine* in August 2008 captured Brisbane's rapid makeover from "ugly duckling" of Australian cultural taste. Demographer Bernard Salt, a regular zeitgeist diagnostician for the paper, set the tone by observing: "Brisbane used to be almost a parody of suburban Australia . . . But now, creative people don't feel they have to leave. It's so exciting because it's come from such a low, flat base." The story was just one arm of the promotional material in the issue feting the third annual "Mercedes-Benz Fashion Festival" – another barometer of the city's upward mobility. Salt hardly hesitated to malign Brisbane's pre-boom image before celebrating the enlightened city emerging with an influx of residents from other states. "These days, it's a bit like a fried egg," Salt described the city. "It has this very dense, funky center stretching around Spring Hill, New Farm, the Gabba and West End, and all of that is cementing nicely."

Such comments again bring to mind Ross's (2008) argument that "creative" cities are successful to the extent that they garner erudite observations about bankable real estate hotspots for investors. The work experiences of actual residents employed in creative industries go missing in these accounts, as do the views of long-term locals loyal to Brisbane in spite of political conditions and speculator interest. In January of the same year, Salt had described Queensland as Australia's "Peter Pan state" given its "ability to draw young, able-bodied workers in droves." The lifestyle city imagined in these stories is a world where the aged, the unemployed, and the poor fail to register. Appearing in *The Australian*, one of few newspapers addressing a nationwide readership, Salt's characterizations of Brisbane revealed a limited set of priorities on the part of non-Queensland readers. With some insight into the city's history, however, his platitudes were further indication of why the creativity agenda needed to be strong. Years of ideological tyranny and entrenched civic corruption had severely damaged outsider assessments of the city's economic potential.

On a local level, the gung-ho positivism of press coverage celebrating Brisbane's transformed night life and boutique shopping districts catered for an expanding inner-city population. Many of these writers and readers had the luxury of choosing not to dwell on the state's tainted past since they had not personally endured it. Brisbane's younger residents, and the migrants that had arrived from further afield, had little need to modulate their views beyond the high-density and high-income lifestyles of the state's south-east corner. The gulf that had always existed between Queensland's north and the metropolitan south only grew in the boom, as commentators spoke of a "two-speed economy." This diplomatic term avoided more antagonistic representations of a situation where city-based office workers could remain ignorant of the radically different conditions of the mining and resource hubs in the far-reaches of the state – and how these traditional industries contributed to their own good fortune in a "creative" economy.

Media sound bites certainly assist in appreciating the speed with which Brisbane moved from a city with little tolerance for diversity to one which promoted such tolerance as one of the hallmarks of a culturally sophisticated lifestyle. Whether "the lifestyle city" had adopted more encompassing attitudes was hardly the issue; ideological change was simply necessary at the level of business rhetoric if the city's most ambitious and energetic workers were to be encouraged to stay. This is because in the space of a decade the lure of creative work had become pervasive in a range of other media formats pitching themselves to young, educated professionals. As the following section illustrates, technology advertising of the same period matched wider efforts to develop Brisbane's profile as the destination of choice for urbane, creative workers.

The rise (and rise) of the frequent flyers

Mobile technology just gets more convenient for international travellers. Most good hotels have broadband and I find my BlackBerry now indispensable, though it's a bit sad when you find yourself reading emails in the middle of the Forbidden City in Beijing!
Traveller Profile, *The Australian Financial Review*, 2007

The vital companion to the leisure affordances of newly minted creative cities is a flexible and fulfilling work culture. This hangover from the dot.com bubble has been the legacy of Baby Boomers coming of age in the US Cold War period who were influenced by West Coast anti-institutional thinking. The marriage of "counterculture" and "cyberculture" (Turner 2006) in figures like Stewart Brand proved a powerful influence on the way that technologies would enter the workplace already articulated to the widespread expectation that work could and should escape the nine-to-five office. By the 1990s, "the same machines that had served as the defining devices of cold war technocracy emerged as the symbols of its transformation" (Turner 2006: 2). As Turner explains it, "the coming together of former counterculturalists, corporate executives, and right-wing politicians and pundits" in influential trade magazines like *Wired* proved an unstoppable alliance in demonstrating the benefits of deregulated, autonomous work cultures (see also Streeter 2010, 2005, 2003). Despite their differences, these groups shared an interest in making work the ultimate manifestation of the good society. The body and mind of the employee would henceforth be geared toward efficiency and diligence with the assistance of new communications platforms.

The significance of this new generation of entrepreneurs was their ability to inspire friends and contacts with the cultural capital to depict them as "emblems of the social forces they chronicled" (Turner 2006: 255). As such "the technologies, theories, and work patterns" of a specific group – research scientists interested in technology – came to be seen as natural for all: they became "cultural rather than simply professional styles" (ibid.). As we saw in the previous chapter, these developments gained traction in the context of a "new spirit of capitalism" which valued self-reliance among workers in decentralized organizations, workers who can be trusted to demonstrate their ongoing employability. Today's creative entrepreneurs thrive by "moving flexibly from place to place, sliding in and out of collaborative teams, building their knowledge bases and skill sets in a process of constant self-education" (Turner, 2006: 7).

Technology advertising circulating in Brisbane in the middle of the decade reveals something of the depth of infatuation with this enterprise culture, including the emergence of an aestheticized work *style*.[11] When this study began, online devices were depicted in a range of advertisements featuring "frequent flyers" clearly benefiting from the convenience of taking the office anywhere. Businessmen with BlackBerrys at the ready were urged to "Pick up your connection as soon as you arrive with Telstra Flexible Networking" in generic airline arrival lounges. Vodafone's "Now" campaign depicted a young woman connecting to mobile broadband from her laptop at a departure gate in line with the slogan: "Check out your email after check in." These emblematic images of autonomous, mobile work reinforced that individuals were free to engage in paid labor without being literally present at the office. To possess the technology was to reflect one's status in the workplace hierarchy, just as it demonstrated commitment to the job. It was also a way to cope with the "down time" and isolation that came with growing experience of work-related travel.

As these advertisements developed in scope, the tone of their appeals became increasingly insistent. Taxi-rank billboards in capital city airports reminded visiting executives they could "get to work before the taxi does," while magazine ads urged workers to "get back to clients from the back seat of the cab." Airline lounges housed billboards with go-get-'em slogans: "20 minutes opening a book or 20 minutes closing a deal?" By 2009, Telstra smartphones were trumpeting their leadership in "turning down time into work time." The sheer number of advertisements of this kind seemed destined to promote obligation, if not also myopia, on the part of traveling employees. In the era of intimate work, to actually enjoy the "freedom" of being away from the office and the surroundings of another city was to breach the expectation of perpetual productivity. Mainstream corporate travel prospered in the erasure of cultural difference and any other obstacles to business.[12]

Telcos and hardware providers were equally concerned to show-case the many non-office locations where work could be performed: a bus stop (Telstra), the bus itself (Vodafone), a cliff face (Sony), the beach (i-mate), a catamaran (Telstra), a building site (Telstra), a park (Bigpond), a cafe (Telstra), a hairdresser's (Telstra)[13] – even nude (Vodafone's BlackBerry Mobile Email bundle). The notion of "transit time" extended from its original context, the frequent flyer lifestyle, to the more generic experience of mobility for the "ordinary" worker. The ostensible appeal of online devices was the ability to "Get to Work Before You Get to the Office." Toshiba's 2005 flexible working campaign (the result of its 2004 research report, "Mobility and Mistrust") encouraged employees to check email at home to avoid peak hour and capitalize on the most productive part of the day. Other advertisements featured a pregnant woman telecommuting from home with the tagline: "Because she's having a baby, not a lobotomy." These strategies, which reframe the home as the place for both men and women to triumph over the challenges of paid work, are part of the wider cultural context for employees' own – apparently individual – reflections in the chapters that follow. The advertisements' emphasis on terms like "convenience" and "flexibility" provided the basis for broader public perceptions of technology in the workplace before their use became mainstream. The positive con-notations of the terms obscured recognition of the fact that access to "unlimited email" at all hours of the day may not be good for all employees, even if it had become a mark of distinction testifying the brand superiority of hardware manufacturers and telco providers.

Unlimited work

Advertisements for the flexible workplace featuring new media tech-nologies stretched in this period to include in-flight magazines, weekend newspapers, and business and current affairs publications. The normalization of online, mobile work cultures took place across a number of fronts: as part of expanded recruitment sections and lift-outs in broadsheets; a similar expansion in the coverage of leisured and work-related IT targeted to both ordinary and executive workers; technology advertising in travel and leisure magazines; and "how-to" guides explaining the steps involved in setting up a functional home office. The latter were found in the midst of bourgeoning real estate and home decorating coverage – part of a wider interest in renovation and makeover style during the financial boom (Allon 2008). Technology regularly featured in a range of "special advertising reports" attached to newspapers. These pedagogical tools not only domesticated new products for a mass audience, but also provided useful content for print publications seeking to boost falling revenue streams in the online era. As lifestyle lift-outs became standard in the popular press, the publicity departments of large tech companies supplied plenty of suggestions on how best to use new technologies at home.[14] With paid-for content passing as story, recruitment and technology supplements were hard to distinguish from buyers' guides. Meanwhile, advertising features sounded like press releases which themselves echoed the instructions for workplace and government policy implementation packages.[15]

The pact between PR companies and lifestyle journalists in the mainstream press was a powerful combination that helped to sell the flexible workplace to a wider constituency in the course of the decade. This mutually beneficial relationship on the part of preexisting media players helps to explain how the more extraordinary possibilities new technologies may have offered quickly turned into something altogether more banal for most workers. The rise in technology lift-outs in major middlebrow newspapers advanced a domestication agenda for new media devices to the benefit of IT companies of all kinds on a global scale. At the same time the glamorization of the lifestyle accompanying these significant changes – epitomized in the "i-Life" suite of Mac products that continued its success throughout this project – concealed the extent to which professional life was being reconfigured to meet the requirements of a networked, information economy.

A Toshiba campaign from 2006 was emblematic of these wider circumstances. The ad featured a closed laptop with an "Office Hours" sign on its lid. The hours listed were:

7.30 a.m.–8.30 a.m.
10.00 a.m.–1.30 p.m.

2.30 p.m.–4.30 p.m.
6.00 p.m.–6.30 p.m.
10.00 p.m.–10.15 p.m.

The copy read: "Because the working day is so yesterday . . . Work out when you work best and when you do your best work . . . Time once wasted in unproductive periods can then be divided between routine tasks, family, friends and fun." The number of hours "working" in this ad – seven and a quarter – perfectly matches the pay rate calculated for the salaried white-collar professional. Liberation from the office will have no impact on the hours worked; rather, wireless portability grants the opportunity to tailor one's schedule to fulfill the usual number of hours expected. Turning to the comments of workers from this study whose experiences form the rest of the book, we can begin to appreciate some of the circumstances overlooked in this optimistic vision.

Miranda, a telco employee who moved to Brisbane from Sydney, was one of a number of people we interviewed who enjoyed a "flexible" working arrangement. Miranda worked from home several days a week and enjoyed the opportunity it offered to balance work and family commitments. She explained how happy she was with Brisbane's relaxed lifestyle, compared to her experience working elsewhere:

> If you go to the Sydney or Melbourne office it's a very different environment to here in Brisbane. In the Sydney or Melbourne office – I noticed this when I first came to Brisbane – you've got to be seen to be doing the hours, whereas here, that's never the case . . . If people are here and they're doing 9 to 5 or 9 to 5.30 or whatever and the job's getting done people don't care . . . In Sydney and Melbourne it's a very different story. People like to be seen, or feel they need to be seen, because it's very competitive environment down there.

Since her manager was based interstate, and hardly knew if she was in the office or not, Miranda was free to choose where she did her work. Asked how her schedule typically played out, she admitted that several nights in the past few weeks had seen her working late into the night, after her husband and daughter had gone to bed. These late-night sessions were a common way for her to manage her paid work, and followed on from the rest of the night's chores – helping with her daughter's homework, making dinner and cleaning up afterwards. The time alone meeting deadlines was ameliorated by television which kept her company in the lounge room. This was the place she chose to work in the evenings because it was distinct from the usual location of her labor during the day: the kitchen table.

The flexible work schedule in the Toshiba laptop advertisement assumes that people are both willing and able to contain their work to discrete times. In the case of women, it cannot reflect the other kinds of labor conducted around the hours recognized as paid work. Nor does it register the cumulative nature of chronic email checking, in and out of the workplace, or the growing phenomenon of incidental or background work. Those we will meet in coming chapters keep their work email running throughout the day and evening. This *ambient* workstyle is illustrated in Miranda's decision to do less challenging work in front of the TV, even if it keeps her up until past midnight. Miranda's experience captures some of the rigidities and impasses that "flexibility" rhetoric overlooks. Working from home does not change the culture of a workplace, which fixes deadlines in advance, or the reluctance of husbands to share the household chores. The flexible workplace facilitated by technology merely enables the opportunity to move long hours around. It rarely closes the lid on work when paid hours have been reached.

Workstyle

The high-paced information workplace glamorized in technology advertising harbors a number of repressed symptoms. These other effects can be found in a persistent number of supplementary features appearing in career lift-outs during the same period of this study. This other set of pedagogical articles explained the benefits of "sitting properly" to avoid "mouse arm," how to cope with "information overload," and how to set up an ergonomic workstation to withstand eight hours sitting at a desk.[16] They share the same territory as the raft of "personal development" packages now available for employees in large organizations. Also evident in the popularity of Merlin Mann's *Getting Things Done* movement and the associated "life-hacking" phenomenon, self-help efficiency regimes redeploy the principles of management gurus dedicated to the vocation of "working smarter, not harder" (Mackenzie 2008).[17] Warnings to "stay under the limit" (don't hoard server space), action email on first sight, and make use of out-of-office notifications are the pop-culture substitute for the lack of formal management guidelines on e-communications. They are also the belated and plainly inadequate response to organizational inefficiencies and the intensification of computer use that later chapters describe in detail.

This chapter's survey of advertising and press coverage of new media technology extends Turner's observation that the initial marketing push to sell communications devices to high-status workers has allowed *their* work styles, preferences, and practices to form the basis for adoption of these technologies on a wider scale. Advertising for mobile media regularly takes for granted the limited privilege of challenging work, in line with wider policy frameworks pivoting on the assumption that all work is "creative." Cisco Systems' 2007 wireless campaign captured the essence of these trends in copy that read: "Inspiration is wireless . . . and nothing is more inspiring than working better, faster and smarter." Another Cisco spread in the *Australian Financial Review*'s *Boss* magazine expanded this theme to declare: "Work is not a place, it's an activity." The picture of a businessman sitting on the ground in an elevator lobby apparently illustrated the notion that: "Inspiration can strike anywhere. Any time. At a desk or across the office."

High-income professionals depicted in technology advertising in this period appealed to a demographic for whom the workplace had become an intimate part of everyday life: a source of status, adventure, and identity. Online technologies were marketed to a class of worker presumed to hold a creative, fulfilling job. It should hardly need stating that this was far from the reality of most employees. For those in mainstream office work, creativity and innovation were allowed on very specific terms when they were valued at all. The connectivity imperative normalized in discourses circulating between media, marketing, and business promoted work styles that summoned a default association between technology, flexibility, mobility, and freedom. These depictions of the creative economy workplace actively displaced any acknowledgment of "the material and technical infrastructures on which both the Internet and the lives of the digital generation depend" (Turner 2006: 261).

> Behind the fantasy of unimpeded information flow lies the reality of millions of plastic keyboards, silicon wafers, glass-faced monitors, and endless miles of cable. All of these technologies depend on manual laborers, first to build them, and later to tear them apart. (Ibid.)

The rise of digital utopianism ensured that other kinds of work beyond the research and creative sectors were kept safely out of view. The humdrum repetitiveness of vast numbers of low-level white-collar jobs belies the glamor of the mobile elite, as does the outsourced labor of assembly-line manufacture and unregulated e-waste recovery surrounding new media devices. If "the techno-utopians of the 1990s denied their dependence on any but themselves," as Turner argues, the creative class of the 2000s only entrenched this flawed ethical horizon.

Appearing alongside policy initiatives targeted to workers in cultural industries, mobile media devices have been central to the "industrialization of bohemia" in a growing number of cities around the globe (Ross 2004, 2009). For a place like Brisbane, looking to update its image as "the lifestyle city," this convergence of factors offered a compelling opportunity. Those moving from interstate could be assured that leaving the rat race of larger cities didn't spell the end of the more desirable features of urban life. On the contrary, the effort to accommodate an articulate and powerful new class bracket led to absences of other kinds. In its transformation from "ugly duckling" to Cinderella of the nation's creative economy, much of what was specific and unique about Brisbane's culture needed to be excavated to make it inhabitable for an elite group of professionals.

> The *necessary* provision of what Florida terms creative-class "lifestyle amenities" – typically realized in publicly and privately financed entertainment and leisure complexes, including upmarket bars, restaurants, urban gyms, climbing walls, road and mountain bike trails, jogging paths, dry-ski slopes, and so on – is now a crucial element of any self-respecting "creative city" strategy, for it is only through such provision (in conjunction with other vital elements such as middle-class "professional" and "executive" housing, arts provision, and distinctive upmarket shopping opportunities) that the all-important creative classes can be attracted to the city. Indeed, it is arguable that in urban renewal strategies the specific demands of the creative class (or those comparably identified) are now being serviced above all others. . . . and (often deliberately) exclude poor and otherwise marginalized social groups. (Banks, 2009: 676)

In Brisbane's boom, a discrete cohort of the population enjoyed the profits. And even relatively recent inhabitants couldn't escape the creeping sense that a new regime of lifestyle performance and surveillance had taken root – one that might compare in its specificity with the state-sanctioned preferences of decades past.

Creativity's limits

The common lament accompanying creative economies is that the winners take the spoils. The star system relies on an entire hidden layer of unspectacular individuals to facilitate and promote the success of an isolated few. This background infrastructure, of course, includes the administrative and organizational support allowing the mobility and creativity of "the talent." Meanwhile, those who do manage to secure work in creative professions – in feast-or-famine cycles – regularly engage in the self-exploiting tendencies that will ensure their ongoing success. In each case, working life amounts to an anxious fate of unpredictable hours and intense pressure, doused with the lingering hope that status and autonomy will compensate for a lack of financial security.

By focusing on Brisbane, the latest darling of Australia's cultural economy, this chapter has offered an insight into some of the absences in creative class theory, including the street-level tensions at play in the shift to post-industrial work and leisure. A fitting anecdote to close the discussion comes from an early morning interview I conducted with one of the workers in this study in early 2009. Pulling up to park outside her period-style Art Deco flat, once sitting majestically atop Kangaroo Point cliffs, I was shocked to see a huge luxury apartment complex had been built to overshadow Sam's building since my last visit. A bunch of manual laborers were sitting around having their tea break on the freshly laid concrete as I walked past for my breakfast date.

When the new complex is complete, from her study Sam will be able to see the yuppies swimming in their lap pool on the other side of the fence. Later in the year, she'll probably see them again in the crowds enjoying the cutting-edge festival program she has been paid to put together. Sam's quality of life has been intimately touched by the economic fortunes affecting her city, as the wealthy creative class has literally moved in next door. On the bright side, this influx of urbane and wealthy residents to Brisbane has directly contributed to Sam's ongoing employment. Her contract had been renewed for another year, and she's developing a fine reputation as an arts worker after a long and lonely apprenticeship. She's also doing an Honors degree in Creative Industries at QUT.

Queensland's branding as the "Smart State" was a fitting amalgam of a much longer hope shared by many other regions – the possibility of an idyllic, harmonious society that could attract and reward talented and motivated workers. What we know now is that this admirable dream was also a practical economic driver that sought to build a better and prosperous future away from the sorrows of the political past. Brisbane's residents, old and new, are now waking up to the prospect that the boom may be over. They would be right to wonder what other values of the place were sacrificed along with the eight-hour workday.

2

Working from Home

The Mobile Office and
the Seduction of Convenience

[T]he worker therefore only feels himself outside his work, and in his work feels outside himself. He is at home when he is not working, and when he is working he is not at home.

Karl Marx[1]

Sorting through an inbox you can do at home sitting in front of the television. I probably wouldn't allocate two hours at work to do that. It would seem wasteful.

Jenny, Library Project Officer

Of all the benefits the flexible workplace has enabled, the recurring feature associated with online technology is the luxury to "work from home." For decades, researchers and employers have offered extensive investigations of this practice from the point of view of workers and organizations alike. Yet, in spite of significant advances in technology over the same period, the shape of these debates has hardly changed in 30 years.[2] Some of the earliest arguments in favor of telecommuting are illustrated in advertisements described in the previous chapter, which show the environmental benefits of working from home and avoiding peak hour. The potential decrease in traffic congestion and the cost of petrol in an era of "peak oil" are major factors driving the push for more flexible work schedules in cities promoting a responsible and sustainable urban lifestyle.

In this chapter, employees explain the factors they find important when choosing to work from home. While some see wider social benefits, including environmental considerations, their reflections are typically more personal, and include regular indictments of office cultures that conspire to create an unhealthy work environment. Ambient lighting, freedom of movement, and lack of stress are among the major benefits cited when working out of the office. The ability to take regular breaks from the keyboard to stretch, make a cup of tea, or move from room to room depending on the task are small affordances indeed, but interviews suggest they are luxuries that the workplace hardly condones.

In contrast to conventional wisdom, it is the enhanced productivity of working from home that many participants claim to be key. At home, workers are able to spend their time wholly committed to the job, as opposed to the workplace, which is full of unnecessary distractions. It's not just the commute that is cut down; workers celebrate the extent to which they manage to avoid *all* interruptions to the number of hours they can be available for work. As later chapters will elaborate, this goes against stereotypical perceptions of working from home that presume domestic temptations are the negative influences on employee efficiency.

Above all, it is the possibility of combining paid work with other tasks and activities – among them interaction with and care for children – that makes employees feel more integrated and happy working from home. The extent to which women name these benefits more so than men (in line with a strong public discourse encouraging them to do so) will be a focus of discussion in what follows.[3] "Working from home" is regularly touted as the solution to women's particular (biologically determined) responsibility to be primary caregivers – as if men had no part in the matter of producing and raising children. The resilience of this double standard, variously justified or excused by the ready supply of part-time work for women in large organizations, reveals how little the gendered protocols of workplace culture have changed in recent decades. Female workers in this chapter describe themselves as "lucky" to be able to combine paid and unpaid work in part-time positions that rarely match the hours of labor. This vocal performance of exceptional treatment, combined with the notion that workplace flexibility is inherently positive, actually disguises the amount of work that remains hidden from remuneration both in their own experience and the broader society.

Making the choice

Of the four organizations chosen for this study, only one had a formal working from home policy. An operational problem with the main headquarters of the broadcaster meant that studio space had to be abandoned. Faced with an office space crisis, a number of workers were offered the option of working from home full-time. Lisa, a 32-year-old radio producer, was one who agreed to the experiment. In 2007 she was on leave from her usual job in radio to focus on developing the broadcaster's online content. Lisa explained that the online department had "grown more rapidly than had been compensated for" in recent times, which exacerbated the space issues already pressing for her employer. Lisa's team was "technically homeless," which made the idea of working from home somewhat attractive.

One of the main difficulties she encountered working from home was patchy infrastructure support, which seemed notable given that her position relied on a significant number of file transfers for stories. Lisa had an intricate array of laptop and desktop computers that she shared with her partner. She used a range of different Internet connections and technical packages according to the task at hand and her own software preferences. This was a complex navigation process given the particular kind of support offered by her employer. For instance, although her work supplied an Air-card to provide Internet access, she found the transfer rate wasn't fast enough to handle the content she needed to upload. This meant she relied on her own home network to transfer files at a decent speed. In effect, Lisa paid for this necessary connection speed out of her own pocket.

Another difficulty was that the network's preferred audio editing software was only accessible internally. Lisa's solution to this was to download freeware to her home computer, since she wasn't authorized to load free software on to her work machine. Earlier in the year she'd been affected by this significantly:

> the computer they gave me was a general use laptop, so it had none of the programs on it that I needed. And so I requested a number of times that I have the software loaded onto it, and it was a difficult situation, because that was when [the broadcaster] had been up and shifted, and the fact that I had a laptop at all was pretty remarkable.

During this period Lisa coped by "loading things onto thumb drives or portable hard drives or emailing things between computers" in the house. This improvised work-around was necessary to meet the clear technical expectations of her role, and is perhaps understandable given the speed with which her employer was dealing with a major operational upheaval. That said, Lisa's story was typical of other workers in the study who also relied on personal networks to deliver work outside paid hours, and few were claiming these expenses. This hidden labor in the home is one of the consistent findings we'll see in the book.

Aside from the pragmatics of file exchange and bandwidth, Lisa enjoyed the experience of home-working. She turned the computer on at around 7.30 a.m., working through to about 3.30 or 4 p.m. She broke up the day by wandering around the house and playing with the dog, but overall she was "very regimented" about focusing on work:

> I would never switch on the television or be distracted with that sort of thing while I'm in work time . . . I won't let anything interrupt it. Even if people call and I've got stuff to do, then they get shafted and I call them back.

Lisa explained her use of email as "particularly anal":

> I think that if I'm working from home, unless I reply instantly, they'll think that I'm baking a chocolate cake or at the coffee shop or something. So I find myself replying really quickly, partly because if you don't, then it disappears in your Inbox and you never find it again, and partly because I'm conscious that if I don't, then it may be perceived that I'm slacking off somehow.

Lisa uses email to perform her competence and diligence for those who are still in the office even though she is not, partly to overcome the perceptions others may have of working from home. Her comments are ironic given the number of advertising campaigns in the previous chapter celebrating mobility and freedom from workplace schedules. For Lisa, email is a barometer of professionalism, just as it was for Jenny, and other workers who worked at home occasionally. "Your email is off? Then how are you working?" is how one telco employee explained her colleagues' regular interrogation.

Lisa only worked from one room in the house, because she suffered shoulder pain without proper ergonomic support: "If I start working anywhere else, it'll hurt!" she mentioned. A health and safety assessment of her office space was promised by her employer when she started working from home, but Lisa decided not to pursue it, claiming: "I'm too frightened that I'll fail." These flouted conventions were mutually beneficial in some ways. The physical symptoms Lisa suffered from working on her computer didn't rate in comparison to the psychological benefits she gained from working away from the studio. "You have more of a perspective," she explained. Being away from the studio context meant that she was less "angst-ridden" about work. Avoiding "a lot of people who are also bitching is probably also good." Ultimately, working from home had brought "a significant improvement in quality of life" for Lisa, "just because I have much more time in my day." She reveled in "no longer having to commute, no longer having to iron" and emphasized that she no longer felt "stressed by work."

Lisa seemed particularly happy to have moved away from the pressure of working in live radio. Working from home allowed her to focus on what she found most important – her job – without the other parts of the industry she didn't enjoy: keeping up appearances, dressing well, and office gossip. The only problem in Lisa's new situation was when she and her partner each wanted to work at home. As a photographer, Ben took freelance work a couple of days a month, and this extra work was reliant on their shared home-based equipment. Conflict would sometimes arise when both of them wanted to be working at the same time. When intimate space is also increasingly workspace, several couples in the study needed to develop tactics to negotiate a shared investment in their job (see chapter 8).

Following our first interview, Lisa took some time out from the study to focus on a new baby. When we met again in 2009, she and Ben had reassessed their arrangements. Lisa was now back working in the office. The revised schedule had Ben staying home to look after the baby during the day while Lisa left for work early in the morning. Starting at 6 a.m. meant that she could avoid traffic grid-lock and reserve plenty of time in the afternoon for playing and feeding her little girl. Meanwhile, each morning Ben would video-phone Lisa at work so that she could see her baby wake up. In the transition from radio work to online content, Lisa's job role had changed to more procedural tasks (for instance, she was writing a guide on how to use the network's website). For the moment, however, this was preferable to the fast pace and giddy egos that seemed a feature of her previous role. For Lisa, working from home had been the circuit breaker to get some time out from the culture of the workplace and return with some new priorities.

Home duties

Richard was an experienced journalist for the same broadcaster who also took the option to work from home. His immaculate two-storey residence overlooking the Brisbane River was a peaceful respite from the remote and often troubled locations he would visit as a news reporter in the Pacific Islands. The change from a studio base involved a considerable amount of organization of Richard's home office, although the size of his house meant that this didn't disrupt the family very much. Richard had a dedicated office in an upstairs room, away from the main living areas. These details are worth noting as we meet more workers in the book, since the choice to work from home often comes down to very material questions to do with space and schedules. Only a certain proportion of the population can ever afford to have a spare room at home to devote to a home office. In this study, those in senior positions – those who owned their own homes and had the financial security accumulated from a successful career – were more likely to see working from home as a viable choice. Younger workers on contracts had few other options. The experience therefore differed according to age and seniority in the workplace. Even within Richard's organization, casual workers living in rental properties had to share a bedroom or living room with their partner if they were to work from home.

As a foreign correspondent, Richard's changed working arrangement didn't prove much of a contrast to the ways he was accustomed to filing stories from the road or hotel room. This is a useful reminder that "remote working" has been common in professions like journalism well before the Internet. As Lisa did, Richard faced technical difficulties since he had started working from home full-time. Previously he had been able to rely on the work studio to process and send stories. Now he depended on his daughter to solve a number of recurring problems with network access on his computer – yet more hidden labor in the home. These pragmatics aside, what Richard missed most about the office was the interaction with colleagues. Even though his closest friends at work were classified in a different branch of the organization, the sense of collegiality he missed came down to the sense of companionship and conversation they offered. Richard lamented the loss of idle chat, about sport and issues beyond the immediate concerns of the workday.

Throughout his career Richard regarded himself as "very much a one-man band," so thinking about his job in terms of location was a difficult process. He saw the role of the journalist as solitary by nature, and when he was away on assignment he rarely distinguished between working and non-working hours. Moving into the home space, fitting his job around others required some finessing. In our first interview, he shared an example of an incident that took place when his wife reacted to him filing stories from the balcony on a Sunday morning:

> Rachel was furious with me, one day, and I got upstairs and I was editing, and all of a sudden I could hear all these bottles banging and crashing in the background and it was her dumping all the bottles in the rubbish bin. I think she was annoyed that I was not only working Monday to Friday, but also working Sundays. Since then, we have now come to an agreement with the network that I have Friday afternoons off.

Before he saw the impact that his work was having on others, Richard hadn't sought to develop any strategies of time management around his work. On the job overseas, "on" and "off" times were artificial distinctions. It was only when returning – both to Australia and the family home as a place for work – that these cultural markers had to be reimposed. Richard was finding he had to learn to express sensitivity to others' needs in the home; to appreciate that his work was becoming part of the family's intimate space. His thoughts on this were instructive:

> The good thing about coming back to Australia is actually this expectation of people in Australia that you deserve two days off a week, whereas for some reason, when you're overseas, when you're a correspondent, nobody has that courtesy. You're expected to be there, available, and when everything happens, to drop everything and do it. If you're actually based in Australia, it's strange, because it's not as if I'm closer to anyone, but there is this belief that you need two days a week off, which is not what any foreign correspondent expects or gets treated like.

Unlike other workers in the study, Richard had extensive experience living and working in another culture. In this context, he performed a role that had no expectations of time off. This gave him a degree of perspective on his job that younger workers tended to lack. The main difficulty he found working from home was adjusting his entrenched habits to the preferences of his partner who had different ideas about work's intimacy. With this new arrangement, Richard's job was giving him more time together with his wife than either of them had been accustomed to. This called for changes to some of their previously established domestic arrangements, since both of them being at home all the time risked a degree of overexposure. As new grandparents, one of the changes that had been instituted was that Rachel would go and babysit for their son two to three days a week, so that she could "get a break" from Richard. In general, though, Richard's arrangement was proving positive, once these teething problems had passed: "I've been rather pleased with how it is has operated," he mused. "I'm not quite sure what I was expecting, but I think it's worked out better than I thought it would."

Keeping in touch

These two stories are helpful for showing how working from home can suit certain personalities better than others. Richard and Lisa both enjoyed the autonomy that working from home offered, at least during a particular stage in their career. But the wider experience this book documents is that of the mid-career majority: those who work from home every so often depending on their current work-load. Here the rationale is to recognize the number of employees now regularly working from home as a matter of course, whether or not this is acknowledged by their employer. The availability of online technology in middle-class homes has been part of the context by which "keeping in touch" with work has become commonplace, even unremarkable, in many ordinary office roles. What's also inter-esting about this phenomenon is the way in which employees con-sistently justify the need to stay in touch with work because their job is exceptional in some way: "it's the nature of project work," "in this job you have to be committed," "that's the life of a journal-ist," etc. As preceding chapters have suggested, it is no longer simply the "creative," cutting-edge or highly paid positions that require an always-on dimension. Rather, it is typical in the most mid-range and ordinary kinds of information jobs regardless of status or financial compensation.

The prevalence of this *incidental* home-work was epitomized during the recruitment phase of the *Working from Home* study. Asked if they worked from home at all, potential participants would often say no to begin with. Asked if this included reading email, however, they would regularly admit that yes, they *did* do that. The very fact that people disregarded email – literally did not count email as work – was an index of the problem I sought to investigate. Checking email was the work that dare not identify itself as such. "It's not even work; it's bullshit work. It's deleting email!" said journalist, Patrick. Wendy, an executive producer in television, agreed: "A lot of it's crap – it's like 'yes', 'no', 'thank you', 'I've done that – thank you' or 'thank you for thanking me'. I hate it – I actually hate email." Even though workers admitted that managing high volumes of email was a perpetual drag on their time, they hesitated to assign it the category or status of "real" work. Email maintenance took place alongside all kinds of domestic and leisure practices, like watching television.[4] The main reason given for the behavior was that it would be wasteful to catch up on email in paid work time.

Workers in mid-level roles showed a particular willingness to engage in extensive regimes of preparation and recovery before and after hours spent in the office. These anticipatory practices were an effort to smooth the way for the priorities of the formal working day. Such diligent techniques of monitoring also eased the possibility that anything surprising might occur in between appearances at the office. Susan, a 37-year-old mid-career university lecturer, explained: "I start at about half past six in the morning and do an hour or so before I leave to go to work and that's mainly just clearing emails and things like that so I can start the day ready to do 'work'." Tanya, 41, a project officer, had arrived to 100 emails in her inbox on the morning of our interview. She admitted that: "Sometimes I'll get into that habit of checking my emails before I come into work. You can spend ages doing that . . . It's often checking to remind myself to see if I've got a meeting or something early Monday, to make sure I get here on time." Her colleague Donna also acknowledged: "it's probably more out of habit now . . . and I guess being prepared for my week, yeah it's more of a habit . . . than a necessity, so yeah. It's my own fault." The personal blaming evident in these responses was a familiar refrain across age groups.

Clive, a 61-year-old university professor, diagnosed his problem with eloquence:

> I think I'm a bit too either addicted or compulsive about it or obsessive about it . . . I worry that I'm going to miss something that I ought to be attending to, and I worry that if I leave it for a day, then I'm going to come back and then I'll just have 60 or 70 emails at the end of the day . . . So to that extent my emails are completely Sisyphusian. It's just never ending. It's like my To Do list. I'm down from 70 things to do on my To Do list, to 30, but that 30 keeps on – it's a perpetual 30.

Like others, Clive checked email at home because "otherwise it would just get on top of me":

> I think I'm a bit email obsessive. I'm a bit addicted. Partly because I don't want email to swamp me. If I have a weekend off the Internet, then on Monday, I have just a huge mailbox.

Workers were concerned that they would start the week "on the back foot" if they didn't check their Inbox on weekends. By spending time clearing mail at home they could get on with proper work once they got in – "hit the ground running" as one person explained.

For part-time workers, this practice extended to checking email on the evening of days off "just to see" what had been missed. Laura, a part-time instructional designer, told us that after her regular Thursday off: "There is usually a lot of emails that I have to deal with when I get back on that Friday morning and they take up work time." So at the end of her day off she would "have a little whiz through and check so I know what to expect the next day." As the study progressed, and it became apparent just how many people were engaging in this practice across industries, it became the basis for follow-up questions. Asked what would happen if she didn't check her email, and actually took the full day off. Laura replied: "Well, I would just be surprised when I got to work on Friday morning and found out all the things that had been going on. I would just be a bit less prepared, I think, for what I have to do." The importance of being "prepared beforehand" for the work "missed" during her day off meant that Laura took individual responsibility for her part-time hours. As the previous chapter indicated, the flexible workplace allows changes to the scheduling of work, but has little effect on the amount of work to be completed.

What seems vital about the home space is its capacity to allow workers to feel "mentally prepared" before arriving at the office for a normal day. The emotional labor of professional performance apparently requires the development of psychological strategies that will allow some sense of control over an unpredictable situation. With email, the medium is never the message: workers never know, opening their inbox each day, just what it is they can expect to find. The anxiety that comes from anticipating the highs and lows to be found in email, and the sheer number of messages potentially waiting, are two of the major "anticipatory affects" of contemporary knowledge work.

The remarkable aspect of this checking behavior is that workers acquiesce to a degree of diligence that is in no way rationally rewarded. In their view, the problem is not that there is too much email; rather it is that email takes up time. And it is work time that is seen as the most precious time that email takes. A lack of institutional guidelines for email use in the organizations this study covered directly fed such ambiguous attitudes. Workers felt unable to "count" email communication as work because it had never been widely discussed in workload terms. This is in spite of its centrality to so many job roles.

The catch-up day

If full-time workers in the previous section feel the need to use home networks to keep in touch with their email, Laura's experience highlights the dilemma this poses for part-time workers in information- and communication-heavy workplaces. Claire, a 33-year-old marketing professional, also chose to work part time. Aside from a four-year stint working for a telecommunications company in the UK, Claire had spent most of her life studying and working in Brisbane. Returning from Britain to work in a similar role, she and her partner had also decided to have children. For the first two years of the study, Claire was working three days a week in the office and looked after her son on Thursdays and Fridays. Claire described these as her "catch up days":

> Thursday and Friday are my days off, but at the moment [. . .], I'll be setting up a meeting for Thursday, and typically Thursday morning is a bit of a catch-up morning for me anyway to send out a lot of emails and get a lot of things moving so that I don't have to wait until Monday before I can get momentum happening on things.

Without this extra work, Claire thought that her return to the office on a Monday would be "really stressful. Yeah, and that's why I do it; it's not because there's pressure from the management team to do it at all, but it's more just for my own sanity." Claire explained her arrangement as "about me being in control," even though by the time of our second meeting the amount of work she was doing outside the office had increased. Whereas initially it was just a case of keeping an eye on things during her day off, only "occasionally doing that extra bit," in the space of 12 months it had become "pretty regular." She emphasized that:

> Management would never expect me to be online, you know. But it's more just if I don't, like if I've had a really crazy day of meetings, like yesterday, and there were so many back-to-back meetings, and I just knew my email was out of control and I had things that I needed to get done, I will sleep better if I spend an hour or an hour and a half at night just getting on top of that, otherwise I will wake up at

4 a.m. in the morning and I'll be just spinning around my head. Got to do this, got to do that. So yeah, for my own sanity.

Her husband Scott was a mortgage broker, and quite often they would spend evenings "sitting on our couch with our laptops on our laps doing work." While in our first interview she was joking that this was a bit unfortunate, by the second year she'd decided:

> it's just sort of something that we've realized for both of us, that just keeps us sane. So it's not that that's all the time we spend together, but I suppose we're lucky with our son . . . he'll be in bed at 7.30 p.m., so then you're right for the night if you do want to catch up on a bit of work as well as relax.

What's interesting about Claire's story in relation to others in this study is the arrangement of the sentence. It's relaxing to be able to catch up on work together. It's a way of being at peace and at ease with the family. For Claire, the home is a site for various kinds of labor, care, and leisure, often in close proximity. Opportunities for paid work are seized in the few unscheduled moments of her day. During her days off, wireless Internet allowed Claire to work anywhere in the house, so that: "if we are out the front playing cars with my two-year-old on the driveway I can still be doing a bit of work as well." Claire sought strategies to limit being on the computer "when I should be giving my son attention," but she figured: "if I can sort of juggle the two and still be rolling cars down the driveway or playing fire engines, then that's OK."

There were times when Claire had to be quite firm about the limits of her contact with work. For instance, "quite often on a Friday I will actually just turn off the laptop and it will still sit there but it will be turned off so I am not tempted to go and check it." These comments suggest the convenience of the device contributes to her readiness to engage with work so readily. Claire needs strategies to withstand the "temptation" of her laptop connection. This is another way we might want to consider work's intimacy. The coerciveness of communications technologies is their capacity to enhance a pre-existing psychological connection to the job, just as the convenience of the devices allows work to take place in more and more places. Whether or not Claire does work on her laptop, its presence in the home is a material reminder of work's potential, and this reminder is occurring in a growing number of places around her house. "I don't do a *lot* of work from the bed," Claire went on to tell us, but she had enough experience doing so to acknowledge that sometimes "you suddenly realize you've been sitting there for three hours and gosh my back hurts."

Lucky mummies

Claire was one of a number of working mothers in the study who felt grateful for part-time hours:

> I do feel very thankful to be able to work part time with my sort of job. It is not really typical that you can do a project-based job and only be there half of the week. It is not a transactional thing. So I feel very thankful and that's why I want to make it work and I don't mind working extra on those other days, particularly just keeping an eye on things so that it works.

While Claire considered her arrangement to be somewhat exceptional, her experience corresponds strongly with part-time employees in other organizations. A sense of reassurance was shared by working mothers who relied on home Internet connections to keep track of work or finish things they didn't have time to do during office hours. Tanya, the project officer from earlier, explained:

> I'd like to think that I could just leave it all behind, but when it is really busy I'd feel a lot more stressed when I'm here if I didn't know that I have access at home. Because I leave sort of early and then sometimes if I haven't finished something I'll finish it at home, that day.

Tanya's description of leaving "sort of early" obscures her status as part time. She regularly worked through lunch to maximize her productivity during contact hours, but often still couldn't finish the tasks required on a typical day.

A further and related rationale for working from home was that there was simply no one else to do the job. Rather than seeing this as a management issue, for instance, Tanya saw her circumstances as "just the nature of the work world today." She was adept at making excuses for co-workers who seemed to forget her part-time status. In the time between interviews Tanya had even approached her supervisor to ask for her workload to be reviewed, but she was still having difficulties in our second meeting. Overall, she believed her conditions were very good, and so she was unlikely to raise the issue again. "I feel like you ask so much," she said, "and you think, well, I better not ask any more."

Jenny, the project officer we met in the Introduction, worked part time for the library as well. Despite her formal paid hours, she also took responsibility for the deadlines maintained by others:

> I finish work at 2 o'clock on a Wednesday and a Friday, but I will often still at 5 o'clock just log in and check my emails, because if something has come through that just needs a quick draft, I'd rather deal with it and get it out of my inbox before Wednesday.

Jenny maintained that it is her "own style" to keep up with her email outside work; it is her personal preference that makes her "happy to take 10 minutes out of my day at home and check." Like other employees who demonstrate anxiety about the potential of work, she says "it's because it almost gives me a peace of mind that I don't have something really big waiting for me." The structural dimensions of the workplace press intimately into Jenny's daily concerns, causing her to take time out to check back in to the office. Her fear of "something really big waiting" is an indication of the unpredictability she must factor in to her individual routine.

A third part-time employee from the same organization, Donna, justified working from home because "it's the nature of project work" to have 5 p.m. deadlines. As a project coordinator, this meant that she would regularly log in from home to receive and respond to messages by the opening of business – in synch with full-time colleagues. Even though management "probably wouldn't openly say we encourage you," Donna argued, "it is an understanding that you will do that."

Working from home is taken as inevitable by each of these women. Even though their language speaks of personal preference and exceptionalism, their consistent stories point to a clear problem in the way part-time work is recognized in information and communication jobs. No formal policies existed for them to manage online obligations; nor were there guidelines for appropriate response times. Employees operated on the basis of vague and self-imposed ideas about what management would or wouldn't expect. In each case, there was simply no framework for discussing how part-time work was repositioned in light of the widespread reliance on online technologies in team-based office cultures (see chapter 4). Technology served to confirm, when it did not also accelerate the temporality of the workplace. Improvised and makeshift arrangements left many part-timers feeling apologetic for their so-called "flexible" positions. Across different workplaces they navigated the perceived expectations of others individually, only sometimes managing to develop strategies to share extra work among other women in the same position.

The cost of convenience

Mums already do ten jobs on the go! Make it easier with a Windows Mobile 6 smartphone.

Windows mobile advertisement,
Good Weekend Magazine, 2008

Interview material described so far shows the home to be a consolatory space stretching to accommodate the limitations of contemporary work cultures. Online technologies allow the encroachment of work-related communication at the same time as they provide a psychological buffer zone to anticipate the move between intense and consuming office schedules and the comforts of domesticity. For women and men, paid work is one of a range of tasks scheduled into the dynamics of the modern home. And yet, Marx's formative definition at the beginning of this chapter continues to cast a shadow over attempts to theorize the domestic support structures behind the online, networked, knowledge economy. Of course, for women, the home has never been synonymous with leisure (Oakley 1974; Barrett 1980; Fortunati 1995; Huws 2003). For women engaged in professional careers today, it is the site for many competing forms of physical, administrative and affective labor. In many cases, the opportunity to balance these incompatible roles is accepted with gratitude, as if it is the pinnacle of feminist accomplishment and workplace equity; as if no better solution could be imagined for the requirements of contemporary work. In starting this project, my hope was that the influence of feminism – combined with the aestheticization of mobile work outlined in the previous chapter – might bring changes to this gendered experience of home-based labor. The sheer presence of men in the home, with the advancement of remote networking technologies, might be grounds for optimism that the domestic division of labor may change as well. As we've seen, there is certainly some evidence that improvements are underway. The father who stayed home to look after the new baby led to a more healthy situation for Lisa. Richard was one of a number of male participants who found new ways to interact with his wife and children while working from home. But by far the most common experience was the multi-tasking, mid-rank, anxious working mother whose commitment to work and home pushed every day to the limit. Her use of online networks was governed by twinned feelings of responsibility: on the one hand, to stay in touch with a workload forever off-course; on the other, to attend the needs of a family that paid dubious recognition to her labors.

For these women, the boundaries between labor and leisure, work and home have blurred to such an extent that it is no longer possible to describe what actually *counts* as work. Any concept of labor limits is abandoned for the more pressing concern to "keep things moving" and "keep sane." For working mothers with childcare duties, online technology is therefore a seductive convenience. The increased potential to work from home to maintain professional credibility creates a heightened sensitivity to the number of productive hours available in any given day. Time becomes a resource easily wasted, as home space is assessed in terms of efficiency regimes and scheduling potential.

During the course of this study, a multitude of images appeared in mainstream media depicting women effortlessly attaining "work–life balance" through mobile devices. By contrast, women's actual use of technology indicated that such models are among the most unsatisfactory models for sustainable workforce participation. In double income families, women moved between various phases of a never-ending working day, with only a fraction of this time compensated financially. Meanwhile, those who did enjoy working from home claimed to do so because it prevented the distractions of human contact. Working from home successfully reflected the consensus in popular business press coverage trumpeting the productivity benefits for workers and employers alike.[5]

What must be acknowledged is that women's decision to perform paid work at home beyond their contracted hours makes it difficult for their employers to register. When this work is also conducted in the witching hour of late-night sessions and pre-dawn email schedules, as subsequent chapters will explain, such recognition is even less likely. Women's acceptance of their ascribed role as homemakers and caregivers leads directly to this second or third shift (Hochschild and Machung 1989), making them complicit in perpetuating the home as the primordial site for their labor. Women's extended history of working from home prepares them well for the mobile, multi-tasking, high-paced environment of the contemporary workplace. In fact, their decision to engage in work at home might be read as further testimony to their innovative resourcefulness: a response to the *lack* of flexibility in workplaces which proffer a range of obstructions to getting the job done. Working women's desire to be productive certainly marks them as the ideal employee for contemporary capitalism, as other feminist commentators have noted (McRobbie 2007, 2009). The following chapters provide ample opportunity to question whether they may be proving a little too efficient for their own good.

3

Part-time Precarity

Discount Labor and Contract Careers

I think having other people around is really important, having lights
on somewhere else in the building.

Sam, casual radio journalist

The actions of workers discussed so far in the book can be explained
at least partly in terms of their ongoing or salaried status. Once
a pay scale surpasses timesheet surveillance, there has long been
an expectation upon workers that they will perform duties when
and as required. In many ways this is the trade-off for the security
of ongoing employment and protection from economic fluctuation.
In the contexts that will be discussed in the following chapters,
however, the justification for such commitment loses force. A significant feature of the flexible information workplace is the fixed-
term contract, where candidates are hired repeatedly and at short
notice to deliver specific tasks vital to the functioning of the organization. The security of ongoing employment eludes these workers,
despite their ongoing and important contributions, and yet there
is pressure on them to perform to a standard that is proven and
reliable – if not for their current boss to recognize, then to build
a portfolio for prospective employers. The categories of "casual,"
"contract," or "sessional" staff are purposefully constructed to
prevent the benefits of salaried work, whether this means sick leave,
superannuation contributions, or continuing employment following
pregnancy. Beyond these structural aspects, contract workers also
experience differential treatment on a range of micro-levels. As this

chapter shows, an accumulation of these indignities can heighten antagonism toward an employer, leading to feelings of worthlessness and anxiety among workers at the beginning of their professional life. In some industries, it can lead young workers to leave altogether.

Extended work hours have particular consequences for junior employees in the information sector, the "white-collar apprentices" juggling multiple work/study profiles in preparation for a career. Since their relationship to the workplace is on the whole more ambivalent than others, contract workers and casual staff also enjoy relative freedom to express anxieties typifying the wider culture. This is their value to the present study. The experiences of white-collar apprentices reveal the mechanics of organizational life at their most blatant, while also highlighting the contradiction at the heart of professional work today. The hypocrisy of organizations that continue to ask for loyalty, without the reciprocal obligation of security and recognition of service, is the unspoken truth that contract workers help to articulate, and that salaried staff might well heed.

"People don't really care": working at the margins of the organization

Tegan was a 25-year-old university administrator who had been hired as part of a new environmental strategy in 2007. As coordinator of the program, she worked casually (14.5 hours a week) on a 12-month contract and was also finishing a degree in Environmental Management at the same university. Tegan's job required just two days a week on campus, although she had some say over when she worked those hours. Her role was to train the delegated "Green Officers" across the three campuses of the university and answer questions as they arose. A key task was to carry out assessments of workplaces in terms of energy efficiency and waste management.

With environmental concerns a growing priority for organizations over the past decade, one of the biggest issues in Tegan's job was its sheer newness. In initial stages, she encountered a lack of clarity as to what was expected of her. It quickly became apparent that there would be little formal training or induction for her role. Indeed, when she started the job, she thought her boss was "being a bitch to me in general" and was almost ready to quit. Tegan explained that her supervisor hadn't taken the time "to really teach me anything":

> It was like I didn't know how to do shit and I knew I didn't know how to do shit but I was very passionate about the job. But I didn't necessarily know like technical stuff and I didn't know how to do it but no one was there to really support you or help you or teach you. It was like, well, this is what you do and you figure out how to do it.

This lack of definition was hard to negotiate as a junior member of staff:

> I was expected to figure out things and it's quite a complex kind of program and I didn't get like the necessary training to be able to do my job properly. Then there was no support when I needed it anyway. Like my bosses weren't prepared to help me and made me feel like I should know what I'm doing. But I didn't know what I was doing.

This lack of supervision and training reflected the newness of the program itself, although other factors contributed to making the conditions worse. In spite of the negligence she felt in terms of learning her job role, Tegan faced an almost contradictory amount of surveillance through her use of technology. She was particularly frustrated by the fact that her boss had access to her email account and could read messages sent to her address. Tegan's superiors justified this access since she was classified as casual, and messages may require action while she was away from work. But given that the email address used her personal name, and not a generic account label, she felt this to be an intrusion on her identity. This shared email structure also meant that Tegan couldn't check her work email at home, even though she was willing to do so in order to respond to requests in a timely manner. For Tegan, working from home and flexible work practices were luxuries her workplace did not extend because of her contract position, and were part of the reason she left the organization for better options.

Smart casuals: Care without responsibility

For other casuals, the ability to leave email at work was one of the few ways of controlling the invasiveness of communication that arrived at all hours of the day. Angela was a sessional lecturer and part-time PhD student coordinating an undergraduate social science course in 2007. She faced serious difficulties managing the demands of students, who "can email at whatever time that they like . . . they email you on a Sunday or late in the evening or really early in the morning . . . whatever bizarre time." Despite being paid by the hour to give lectures and tutorials, Angela's students had little regard for her casual status, expecting messages to be answered in timeframes more suited a salaried staff member. Of course, as preceding chapters have shown, it is salaried staff answering emails at all times of day and night that confuses the notion of formally paid hours of work. The knock-on effects of this practice for those employed less securely within the same organization are rarely recognized.

Vince, tutoring in a different faculty at the same university, also expressed concern about student expectations. "Throughout the year, it's generally not too bad. But the end of the year, the last week, a student came and was asking me questions for an hour . . . That's a pretty substantial chunk of time." As is the practice in many universities, these tutors had consultation time "factored in" to their hourly marking and class preparation rates, which didn't actually translate to the amount of communication students expected after class, in person and through email. "I guess there's measures in place," Vince reasoned. "Like you can send them off to the lecturer and stuff like that. But I don't know. If you're interested in teaching, then you want to be involved in things like that."

Casuals working in jobs with a mix of salaried and contract positions here face pressure to maintain the communication standards of full-time colleagues. This is especially the case as universities appear unwilling to provide sufficient means to differentiate between staff members according to their employment status.[1] In the absence of any policies directing casuals' online communication requirements, Angela improvised strategies to cope with email contact that exceeded the amount of compensation awarded her role. With multiple jobs during her PhD candidature, this situation was difficult to manage. She admitted to deliberate efforts in delaying responses to particularly needy students.

Aside from lecturing, which required her to prepare classes most weeknights and into her weekend, Angela also worked part time for a welfare rights agency. This second job related to her scholarly interests and was more useful experience for the work she sought after her PhD. This second job had the additional function of allowing Angela to escape the relentless requests of students – to avoid the psychological impact of their emails. She enjoyed being physically away from the pressure to check her university email two days a week and spoke of the sense of freedom this gave her. The irony, of course, was that her escape from one set of work problems came only through the distracting demands of another job.

The isolation casuals felt in relation to the larger organization employing them was underscored by their experiences working with

technology. Entering a lecture theater as a 26-year-old course con-
venor made Angela keenly aware of her lack of training. She felt
stressed at the prospect of technical glitches occurring in lecture
theaters that had no on-hand backup support. Writing lectures at
home on her personal laptop, when Angela would arrive for class in
front of hundreds of students the next day there was no guarantee
that her equipment would work. She had learned to take the IT
support officer with her to the lecture theater "when my confidence
is very low."

For Angela, sessional teaching was characterized by long periods
of isolation punctuated by intense scrutiny from students, whether
through the influx of urgent email or the public pressure of the
lecture hall. Her relationship to the university itself was atomized:
"no one really notices when you turn up or when you leave or cares.
It's really not surveilled . . . just an indifference. People don't really
care." The main reason Angela kept using the shared office workspace at uni was so she could continue to access fast broadband.
If she worked any more from home, she worried that even the
meager cubicle space provided for PhD students "might be taken
away from me."

Without much collegial interaction, Angela often ate lunch alone
at her computer looking up celebrity gossip and other kinds of "recreational interneting." Technology provided the solace missing from
physically present colleagues, as subsequent chapters will show to
be the case with others. But the flipside for Angela was that the same
technology also provided the main "face" of the organization – a
point of access and address. Encounters with colleagues through
email were often negative: the "terseness" of administrative demands
added to the tension caused by students' incessant emails. When she
was upset by this use of email, Angela tried to avoid retaliating in
any way that might express her feelings:

> what I'll do is I'll write the sort of draft angry email, and then for-
> tunately go, no, I really shouldn't do that, I won't send that – I sort
> of get it out through a pretend email and then try not to be angry
> back. But I have definitely sent irritated, with irritable tone to stu-
> dents, really problematic ones.

Like Tegan, Angela was left to negotiate the university bureaucracy
on her own, whether at home or in the office.

Sam, the arts worker we met in chapter 1, had a similarly lonely
time in her first paid job. Finishing her degree, Sam had scored a
boutique job as a casual reporter for a radio broadcaster. Her task

was to file one local arts story a fortnight for a flat fee of $100. But, as Tegan also found, the funding stream that provided Sam's position amounted to a fashionable organizational initiative. It was poorly resourced to minimize risk and the requisite training proved inadequate. Sam found it easiest to come in to work in the evening or on weekends to file her stories because she found it hard to compete for studio time during regular hours. As a casual, Sam wasn't given a login password for the computer she needed to export the audio to produce her stories. This meant she had to borrow a password from a colleague in order to use the right equipment, and the password would often change for security reasons. If Sam was locked out of the hardware, there was no onsite tech support for the hours she worked – usually between 7 p.m. and midnight. This was a genuine problem since the technology she'd been trained for only worked on certain facilities in the studio. To make matters more complicated, the audio software used by the national radio station (ProTools) didn't match the kind used by the local branch of the broadcaster where she was based (Netia). The separate systems led to a range of potential problems when stories were sent interstate for screening, as this story illustrates:

> So I would be here after a University day . . . trying to put something together and often it would just sort of happen that like a piece of it would be missing. I'd sort of be editing and then I'd go back to the early part and I would sort of refer to it on the line to my producer and say there were these phantom pieces, where this piece of audio put there wasn't there anymore and it wouldn't let me put another piece of audio there, because for some reason it was blocking that. It was awful at the time. You just feel really powerless and upset and it could be really, really hard. There were points where I would sort of dread coming into this studio because it could be really anxiety provoking in terms of whether I was going to do five hours of work and then have it all sort of disappear.

Adding to Sam's fear about losing work was the concern that she already worked far longer than she should have to make the stories. When she took the job, she thought $100 per story was justified since "it was sort of like a cadetship in some ways." But over time she realized:

> it was taking me up to 10 to 15 hours to cut a piece and then you have to do the write up so that's a couple of hours and then there's the sourcing and the field recording and so . . . yeah you would sort of feel like if you're being paid $100 for a piece you should be able

to achieve it in a certain amount of time. And I really felt that I just couldn't. It would just take a really long amount of time in the studio to achieve that.

Technical problems meant that Sam often had to think of other ways to file the story. One solution was to try to burn a disk and Express Post it to Sydney by the due date. But given that she worked outside of business hours, she couldn't use the office stationery to make this happen overnight, and would have to pay for the package herself out of her $100 pay check:

Yeah, and even then, sometimes for some reason this software isn't particularly good at burning. You can try and burn something and it won't even burn and then you're worried about missing a deadline. So you have to come in and miss some hours out of your paid working day in order to try and fix up the situation that you couldn't fix up that evening, because there was no technical support staff.

The obstacles Sam encountered in her job were remarkable, yet she was conscious of its benefits. The skills she gained in HTML, sound editing, software, and even email use were valuable additions to her Arts degree:

I mean for the first year [it] was really exciting in and of itself and I didn't have the skills and I was gaining the skills and that was fabulous. And then after about a year it was sort of like well I have the skills to do this now and thank you for that but you're now underpaying me.

The job quickly outgrew her capacity and experience, which reinforces the lack of foresight in planning the initiative. This was in contrast to Tegan's case, where the Green Office program doubled in size during the course of her contract. But both workers suffered from a lack of surveillance as to whether their pay adequately reflected the hours worked.

Later chapters will help to assess whether these alienating experiences of casual work actually act as sound preparation for the flexible, multi-tasking, web-based workplaces typical of information jobs today. For the moment, their stories reflect those of many junior employees whose elongated apprenticeships are at best a CV-filler to move somewhere else. In their mid-twenties and older, with university degrees in hand, their jobs lack the security, mentoring, or even adequate financial compensation that are the basis for many salaried professionals' sacrificial labor. Instead, the employer's brand name serves as cultural capital to trade up to further job opportunities that will hopefully prove more rewarding.

The student worker

A protracted student identity is one reason these junior staff tolerate the circumstances of their workload. Study takes place alongside and in addition to work obligations, making the overall number of hours devoted to career pursuits comparable with older, salaried staff. This present fate of multiple commitments is assumed to be passing – an investment that will lead to more predictable and secure employment some time down the track. But from another perspective this situation may actually mark the beginning of a much longer experience these workers are learning to navigate. The second time we met Tegan, for instance, she had left her university job and was working from home as a consultant for a Melbourne-based company. This new position still accorded with her environmental beliefs, since it cut down on the number of flights the company made to Brisbane to meet clients. Yet the new freedom to work from home brought other kinds of complications, namely, how to manage multiple pressures on her time. She told us she was "trying to work only for the 45 hours a week, because I'm trying to finish my Honors thesis and also work another job":

> This is my final semester of uni so that's really busy, but work is really busy because I started a new project with the Business School, so all the data gathering and analysis is happening now. And with the Melbourne company I guess it's busy because they've got new projects happening, so I'm doing a few hours for them as well. It's a busy time.

It's possible that Tegan could be the kind of girl who is "busy" by nature (just as the working mothers in the previous chapter just happened to be diligent). Still, her regular use of the word is symptomatic of a missing vocabulary that might better describe the conditions of her labor. Accepting work as it arises, fitting jobs around her Honors year, Tegan's experience is one of opportunistic momentum geared toward an elusive period when she will be less "busy." Her workload, like Angela's, comes across as being exceptional, but only for the time being. And like Sam's "cadetship," Tegan's position as a student pursuing tangentially relevant work makes it hard to know when she is qualified and deserving of proper, ongoing pay.

Instead of inhabiting one role with a finite set of tasks, work involves juggling a range of piecemeal requirements in order to lengthen a CV that only *might* generate larger projects at a steadier pace.

So-called "flexible" online delivery modules and night classes on campus are some of the ways university curricula are responding to the changing demographic for higher education. The crossover between scholarship and industry is encouraged through internship programs, PhDs by publication, and recognition of "industry experience" in awarding degrees. But the changing identity of student workers affects their condition in two directions – their access to study facilities and a workplace. Student apprentices in information industries currently struggle to describe the demands and rights of their competing subjectivities, meaning their poor treatment can be dismissed by employers as purely a passing condition.[2]

This "state of exception" influencing young workers' attitudes to labor politics – and universities' complicity in normalizing such attitudes – reaches an interesting climax in another young worker in the study. Patrick was a 24-year-old radio producer and musician employed in morning radio on a part-time contract. He first started at the radio station as an unpaid "work experience" placement as part of a journalism degree. When we met in 2007, working the breakfast shift involved 4 a.m. starts in the studio. Once the program was over, Patrick also maintained a regular amount of media monitoring throughout the day to stay abreast of breaking stories. None of this work was captured by the hours of his contract, but was seen as intrinsic to the job of journalism.

During the course of the study, the breakfast show developed the highest listening audience in its timeslot across the city, a source of some pride to Patrick. The fast pace of the news cycle and the adrenaline of live radio also combined to create a sense of identification with the station, and the job in general. As he put it: "I think it's the kind of job where it's just expected that your life will contribute to the program that you put to air . . . You kind of have to always be plugged in to things that are happening."

While clearly enjoying his job, Patrick was trying to establish some measures to cope with the degree of constancy involved in staying "plugged in." For instance:

> I try not to work right before I go to bed. Apart from just checking what's happening in the news but that's more – I think I do that anyway because I think I'm a little bit paranoid that some place has blown up and I just want to know about it before I go to bed . . . Also I try not to feel like, if I for some reason am not able to see the news

or if there's something that's preventing me from being as connected, I try not to feel too guilty about it.

Patrick's guilt is worth connecting to the thoughts of others in the study who used the same language to describe breaks from work. He was conscious that management encouraged employees to "go out, don't stay at work the whole day, make sure you have a life." But he also thought this was "complete bollocks because there's just so much time that goes into putting the shows together." For Patrick, it was obviously necessary to stay in touch with work at home, but his rare efforts to break free from routine every now and then were justified as: "fuck it, I'm going to go and have a fucking life and not be apologetic about it."

In spite of these comments, from my observation, Patrick hardly ever refused additional work when it was offered. As a part-time employee, he would regularly amend the specific hours he was paid to work by helping out with big events: end-of-year concert "duties," a secondment to set up emergency preparations for the cyclone season, and a new magazine round-up in addition to his usual producing role were just some examples over the time of our interviews. These extra tasks seemed unremarkable to Patrick, perhaps because they were ways to show his involvement in the organization. This commitment was also evident in his willingness to move between early mornings and day shifts, indeed combining them when required. He would also stay on at the studio after his shift for meetings that suited the schedules of others. As he explained:

> Because I'm only here four hours a day, it actually can be – you know, we get off air at 7.45. I'm scheduled on till eight. If we want to talk about anything . . . it's almost . . . You need to debrief after things. Fifteen minutes is barely enough time to debrief. I usually stay here until at least 8.30, nine o'clock every day. Over the course of a week . . . I mean, if you want to be picky about it, that's like a quarter – I did – I already do 25 per cent overtime every day, over the week. I mean 25 per cent over time adds up.

Leaving aside this extra time, the temptation to stay in touch with work heightened when Patrick came home to an empty house mid-afternoon: "The first thing I usually do is switch on the radio so it's not really switching off at all." His one method for relaxing was to get some sleep during the hours his partner was out, which was "a psychological measure to separate things." Later in the day, however, he would check in with colleagues to start organizing the next morning's show:

you realize that it doesn't really matter how many hours you work here. If you're not in touch outside of work . . . you're going to not really be able to do your job properly. That sort of is a little annoying. I mean it's only annoying if it's not what you want to be doing. I guess – you know, I'm more than happy to do all that stuff because I enjoy working here and whatever. But you know, there are times when you can't be as connected outside of work. I don't necessarily want to be a prisoner. Sometimes you can feel very constrained.

Patrick's thinking in this passage crystallizes the justification of many workers in this study. He is "more than happy" to do the work because he enjoys it. All the while, the feelings of constraint and imprisonment he expresses are equally real.

In terms of this chapter's concerns, there is no meaningful distinction between Patrick's role as second producer on the radio program and the obligations felt by the first producer or presenter – both of whom had ongoing salaried positions. Patrick's identification with the organization matches the commitment of any other staff member. Discussing this during interviews, Patrick wondered if it was because he worked for a non-commercial broadcaster that he was more likely to discount his personal needs for the greater good, if the tradition of public service came in to his thinking. Comparing his rationale across sectors in the study, this certainly has merit. Public-sector employees were more likely to mention wider community values and notions of service as motivating ethics for their work. Yet there was something else that stood out about Patrick's sense of his longevity working for this employer that did not match the reality of his position. For instance, at one point he described the new location for the studio, explaining: "we're not here for long, only another two years." But this timeframe was longer than Patrick's own contract. Questioned further on this tendency to project an ongoing relationship to the workplace, he responded: "I don't see not having a job as a barrier to fulfilling career aspirations." His experience had shown that "if you are right for something . . . they just put you there anyway – you don't need a job. It's almost like it's just a formality." Given the time we were holding this interview – just as the financial crisis was starting to take hold – these were brave words indeed. In Patrick's view:

You should never think that you're irreplaceable, because no one is. But if you are useful enough in a workplace then I think generally you will have somewhere there. And that's another reason why I just haven't bothered to apply for a job. What's the point again? What else do I get from having a job?

Clearly, the benefits of having a salaried role include financial dimensions: holiday entitlements, ongoing contributions toward superannuation, paid sick leave. In direct contrast to the thoughts above, Patrick was also aware that he had no access to long service leave despite having worked for the broadcaster for eight years. This was starting to play on his mind, as he and his partner had ideas of traveling overseas. The pair had little capacity to save or plan for this possibility, however. As a freelance writer, Adam was also dependent on casual contracts, both as a sessional teacher and the occasional (highly competitive) writing subsidy or grant. Patrick referred to his current bind, jokingly, as a consequence of the "intelligence of youth" and blamed himself for a lack of strategic thinking since his initial work experience placing.

Masters' apprentices

The changing opportunities for psychological and financial security in employment across class demographics have been major sites of critique and social protest in recent years (Vanni and Tarì 2005; Mitropoulos 2006). The effects of so-called "precarious" employment are also a matter of growing academic concern (Gill and Pratt 2008; Neilson and Rossiter 2008; Brophy and de Peuter 2007), particularly since universities in particular appear to be at the forefront of trends to hire casuals on a serial basis. In this chapter, unstable and fluctuating employment conditions have been shown to affect "the time of life" for young workers, leading to excessive workloads that rarely gain appropriate recognition or compensation. Too often these conditions have been dismissed as befitting the flighty preferences of a noncommittal "Generation Y" stereotype, hiding the growing economic reality of contract careers across age groups. The impression to be gleaned from media coverage is that "workers have chosen this lifestyle" rather than reckoning with "the fact that many jobs are no longer permanent" (Delaney 2009).

In concluding this first part of the book, it is worth remembering that one of the comforts of salaried work is the pleasure of forming ongoing relationships with fellow workers. Central to these human bonds is the ability to welcome and encourage colleagues' relationships and interests beyond the workplace, to allow for a full and rounded life. Patrick's dilemma was hardly an individual failing attributable to his misguided youth. Rather, it was his misfortune at having entered the workforce at a time when previously secure benefits and opportunities had started to resemble lost rights. Patrick

was caught in a work situation that combined temporary convenience and opportunism with a pace and intensity actively preventing the space he needed to imagine life and work otherwise.
Unsociable hours, changing schedules, inadequate remuneration,
and a lack of paid leave all combined to neutralize his capacity to
plan his career any other way. So accommodated had he become to
a fate of precarity that he saw other employees' fixations on hallmarks of security as unhealthy, if not bizarre.[3]

As the study ended, Patrick risked becoming habituated to the
seasonality and adrenaline of precarious work. His optimism that
he would continue to gain recognition for his work was certainly
admirable, but since the broadcaster had already come to rely on his
willingness to work minimal hours, it was also questionable. In any
case, as we will see with other young workers in the book, the real
concern facing Patrick was whether he may have reached a point of
exhaustion and burnout by the time a permanent position did
become available (cf. Deuze 2007).

Distinct internal hierarchies of privilege exist within the wider
category of information work explored in this book. This chapter
has focused on some of the inconveniences and indignities that
exacerbate casual workers' marginal role in large organizations.
Contract workers are shown to accept these issues and extra
job demands to demonstrate their worth to a company, whether in
the hope of securing a long-term relationship or on the assumption
that the apprentice model still thrives. The next section of the
book will assess the wider impact of this discounted labor when
combined with changes to technology use in recent years. Not only
has flexible contract work contributed to a loss of hours gauged
and claimed by employees, the Web 2.0 bubble has allowed a whole
new horizon for unpaid internships in social media for university
graduates.

The lack of interest, care, and support casual employees receive
from superiors is a serious problem in workplaces that too often
take the short-term bottom line as the key priority for survival.
Organizations simply lack viable management strategies if they fail
to provide the collegial connections necessary to inspire loyalty and
commitment from their most vulnerable employees. Employers regularly rely on the enthusiasm and the diligence of young contract
workers in spite of the material conditions of their labor, and this
enthusiasm has a limit. While few of the workers in this chapter
showed outward signs of disaffection, this is unlikely to be representative of more cut-throat commercial industries in an international market for white-collar jobs (see Ross 2006).

The function creep inherent to contract positions is a constitutive dimension of large organizations. The stories encountered in this chapter prompt us to consider whether the very idea of vocational training for "a" career adequately reflects the current and future workplace – both in terms of the magnitude of dependence on mismatched work hours and the number of years workers excuse their precarious conditions. Multiple opportunities, each considered too precious to pass up, stretch young workers' energy to exceptional levels that are justified because they are seen as temporary. This is the case even when this is the only professional existence they have ever known.

A growing literature documents the depreciation of white-collar conditions in many professional settings (Mosco and McKercher 2008; Liu 2004; Andresky-Fraser 2001). The emerging economic might of countries such as China and India challenges the long-held sense of security among Western white-collar professionals whose jobs now appear ripe for outsourcing (Ross 2006; Amman, Carpenter, and Neff 2007). These forces offer a confronting new landscape for professional work. Far from taking the lead in preparing graduates for its realities, however, universities have been at the forefront of wider industry practice in opportunistic job hiring – including, in the case of PhD students, the dubious rewards bestowed on their own best products. We might even suggest that it is universities' own implication in the propagation of contract careers that is the principal obstacle to discerning the requirements workers need to cope and flourish in emerging knowledge industries. To begin this urgent process of reimagining, then, our first imperative must be to stop misleading students, the majority of whom are already workers, with outdated notions of job benefits they may never see, and career paths that may never materialize.

Part II

Getting Intimate: Online Culture and the Rise of Social Networking

4

To CC: Or Not to CC:

Teamwork in Office Culture

When the restructure happened we did some training to make sure
everyone was on board. So that was a couple of trips to Sydney . . . everyone went ten-pin bowling and then Japanese at the Casino.

Miranda, telco Pricing Manager

The stories of young information professionals in the previous
chapter bring to mind the concerns of Richard Sennett, in *The
Corrosion of Character* (1998), that the values of the modern workplace lead to ethical and emotional "drift." The short-term priorities
of flexible organizations threaten workers' capacity "to form their
characters into sustained narratives" (31) – a condition Lauren
Berlant (2008) has termed the "animated suspension" of life under
neoliberalism. Sennett's work sets a precedent and foundation for
the issues raised in this next part of the book, especially his attempts
to understand "the fugitive quality of friendship" (Sennett 1998: 21).
Sennett sees changes to the workplace as key to a wider sense of
insecurity among individuals experiencing a decline in prospects for
community, which is to say, the chance to act as "a long-term
witness to another person's life." In the previous chapter, Patrick's
sense of feeling "on guard" in his constant efforts to be liked by
colleagues are an illustration of Sennett's suggestion, more than a
decade ago, that we are losing "those qualities of character which
bind human beings to one another and furnishes each with a sense
of sustainable self" (27). For Sennett, "detachment and superficial
cooperativeness" are the necessary "armor" to protect oneself from
the "corrosiveness" of the modern workplace. Here he joins other

writers interested in the psychic structures needed to assume a persona of "corporate cool" (Liu 2004). According to Alan Liu, we are currently "on the scene of the abiding suspense of the contemporary middle class, which is even more structurally contradictory than the original white-collar class of the twentieth century" (2004: 19). Employees who may have been accustomed to seeing their value as accumulated through length of service to an employer are now likely to find such skills secondary to the more cherished traits of "flexibility" and "dealing with change."[1] This is a time when workers are "simultaneously deskilled and encouraged to feel a deep emotional attachment to their work" (Moran 2005: 39).

Each of these writers suggests that notions of loyalty and service are no longer valued in workplaces that offer only temporary housing for upwardly mobile employees on the lookout for the next big opportunity, or "project" (Boltanski and Chiapello 2007). In this chapter, we will have cause to question these claims, and to ask whether they may be slightly misplaced. Interviews with workers indicate that loyalty and service are not in themselves outdated as motivating values. It is rather the recipients of these energies – the imagined audience for workers' labors – that may be at issue. If the flexible, decentralized workplace has freed employees from the omnipotent surveillance of the boss, as previous chapters have suggested, today it is "the team" of co-workers that bear witness to everyday work efforts. The team is the mythically egalitarian playing field in which all colleagues work together, sharing responsibility for the organization. It is one of several coercive dimensions of office culture exacerbated by new media technologies and that this part of the book illustrates.

The perception that other co-workers might be waiting for responses and actions is a recurring reason employees give for logging in to read email outside the office. In this sense, employees like Claire are right when they claim "management wouldn't expect for me to be online," and the fact that so many choose to work anyway confirms that there are other motivations for the practice. But if it is loyalty to the team that governs workers' motivations, what must be recognized is that management strategies are the driver for the notion of "the team" in the first place. As we will see, the team becomes hegemonic in office culture due to its effectiveness in erasing the power hierarchies and differential entitlements that clearly remain in large organizations.

Exploring this further, this chapter focuses on the social dimensions that are part of the workload for professionals in information and communication industries. The obligations of networking functions and entertaining clients have long been a part of white-collar employment, yet the friendly demeanor Carnegie encouraged in the quest to "influence people" has lately been met with more ambitious tactics to develop cohesion in organizations that are forever in the midst of flux. Team-building and bonding exercises are evident in the fashion for corporate retreats and boot-camp initiations designed by a new breed of company-hired "culture champions" (Nicholas 2010). "Human Resource Managers," "change management consultants," and "toxin handlers" assuage anonymity and animosity in the workplace while "fun officers" and "Wow!" departments serve the needs of employees who may never meet the boss or get to know their colleagues otherwise (Ryan 2009; *The Economist* 2010). The enforced intimacy of these programs aims to develop personal connections by simulating a democratic work environment with shared overall objectives. Among the more prominent strategies in this effort are the mission statements that present a vision for the company that workers are invited to affirm through their own professional performance.

Team players

The entrance area for the telecommunications company in this study epitomized teamwork culture.[2] Its main headquarters housed a series of poster boards showcasing inspiring slogans, each a derivative of the overarching company mission: "To know our customers and meet their needs better than anyone else." All posters featured an image superimposed upon two words capturing the essence of the organization. The terms were striking for being so generic, and certainly interchangeable with the goals of any corporate entity. For an Australian visitor, the terms also contained a strong dose of irony given dominant public perceptions of the telco.[3] Inside the terms "Done. Now," a male in business suit, arms raised, could be seen leaping mid-air over a gently breaking wave on a sunny beach.[4] The accompanying line read: "We get done everything we need to do to satisfy customers, and we get it done fast to stay ahead of every competitor." Another image, an underwater still of a group of female swimmers at the commencement of a race, formed the backdrop for: "Compete. Win. Winners are the ones who never stop finding ways to serve our customers better than any competitor. We're not here to compete, but to win." Continuing the sporting theme, another poster had a wheelchair athlete, fists raised in triumph as he claimed the winner's ribbon, illustrating the terms: "Anything. Possible.

We'll do anything to assure our customers a better experience. And here, anything is possible." A final image noticed upon entering the building was "People. Power." A young woman in jeans and T-shirt was shown held up by a sea of hands in a simulated mosh-pit. The tagline read: "People are the power behind [our company]."

The rhetorical function of "people power" in this platitude masked the reality of an organization that offered workers little say in company direction.[5] Ongoing industrial disputes throughout the period of this study confirmed that while people might be the power behind the brand, it was shareholders rather than workers who counted. A singular mission – to increase profit – guided management decisions and employees' experiences alike. Public statements of unification and cohesion were nonetheless useful for public relations purposes, outside the company as well as within. In interviews, variations on the slogans provided neat formulae for workers looking to describe the objectives guiding their work. The solace of these value statements was to absolve workers of the need to generate intrinsic motivations for the job. Repeating corporate mantras that were extrinsically imposed and transparently common sense made identifying with them low risk. The obvious contrivance of HR strategies is in this sense one of their main benefits. It is "their very artificiality which guarantees their success" (de Botton 2009: 246).

In *The Pleasures and Sorrows of Work*, Alain de Botton describes some of the further dimensions and functions of this wider teamwork culture:

> the labored tone of away-day seminars and group feedback exercises allows workers manfully to protest that they have nothing whatsoever to learn from submitting to such disciplines. Then, like guests at a house party who at first mock their host's suggestion of a round of Pictionary, they may be surprised to find themselves, as the game gets under way, able thereby to channel their hostilities, identify their affections and escape the agony of insincere chatter.

HR platitudes are a mechanism by which workers learn to manage and develop relationships within the organization, when and as this suits them. They stand in contrast to the more genuine loyalties to the team evident in many workers' day-to-day commitments.

In the case of Claire, the part-time worker we met in chapter 2, the team is paramount in her description of why she logs in from home on her days off. A sense of responsibility to others motivates her "to keep an eye on what is happening" so that "if anything urgent comes through or things I can quickly flick on I will keep that moving and keep that working." Claire worked for the telco on Monday, Tuesday, and Wednesday, but typically kept the laptop connected on other days, including "most of the weekend." This didn't mean she was "actively working," as she put it, "but I am always keeping on top of what's happening." Claire acknowledged that even though the company was "very good with part-time employment, it's still not the majority of people. And no one else really is going to remember what days you work and what days you don't." Her sensitivity to others' schedules compels her to stay connected: "Even though you've got an 'out of office' on . . . it still can be a bit hard for people." Staying in touch therefore had the twin benefit of being "appreciated by the team and it makes me feel better."

Claire worked with an immediate team of four, but a wider team of 21 in the marketing area of the firm. Her closest colleagues were aware of her hours, but it was the larger group that couldn't always be expected to know her schedule. As she explained: "there will be people there that will send something through on a Thursday and they might need it close of business on Friday. So it is good to be able to – if it is urgent and only I can do it – I can actually look at it or I can make sure it is sent on to the right people." For Claire, leaving work alone until Monday would in this situation be "more stress on me," since she felt that others would be waiting for her reply.

The conviction that "only I can do it" gets to the heart of teamwork's interpellative power, just as it signals the inadequate staffing levels that teamwork rhetoric helps to excuse. Knowing that it is her unique skills that are required to facilitate the smooth running of things, Claire feels called upon to continue offering her expertise outside of work hours. One alternative to this would be a job-share arrangement that paid two part-time workers to maintain the expectations of the role; or the full contingent of the team could come to terms with the actual hours Claire was paid to work. But to do so would involve having upfront conversations about the actual as opposed to the relative urgency of tasks being handled – a prospect that may entail splintering the cohesiveness of the team's shared purpose.

CC: inadequacy – multiplying the message

This potential for team solidarity to splinter was clear in the ways employees struggled to develop email etiquette. In so many cases, workers' biggest technology complaint was the inappropriate emailing practices of others. "Some people are really chronic email users and really overdo it with the email," said project officer, Cynthia. She thought that workflows would improve if colleagues would "go and just talk to people, pick the phone up. That could resolve something that didn't result in 10 emails." Clive also wondered whether people used email so much because it avoided the difficulty of face-to-face contact. It was easier, he imagined, to raise problems with a "faceless person than to actually sit down and have a conversation." For Tanya, the problem with email was that "everybody sort of wants more consultation":

> whereas once you would've had just someone say "You can do this," and maybe you'd ring two people, now you can send it to heaps of people and everybody has to . . . it all gets bigger. You get sent information about everything possibly related to – you know what I mean? So it's made more work in a way.

Miranda was another who lamented the times that "CC" behavior got out of hand:

> The thing that annoys me most, I think, would be if a group email goes out, and then you send a response directly back to the originator of the email – not to the whole group, but to the originator – with a response or question, then they respond back to you, but copy in the world again. That for me is extremely bad etiquette, and that annoys me more than anything. That's my one big gripe.

For Miranda, this was a question of professionalism:

> I think if it is something that warrants the rest of the world knowing about it, you should work with the person, resolve it, and then tell everybody if they need to know. There's nothing worse than being on the end of a group email that you don't really need to know about.

Over time, Miranda had noticed her colleagues changing the way they addressed email in order to enforce multiple stakeholders in conversations. With more and more people learning to filter emails addressed as a "carbon copy," she observed: "Carbon copying has almost gone out the door, because everybody wants you to read it, so they just put it in the To-box." This too was a breach of email courtesy for Miranda: "It does my head in. I hate it. I don't need to know."

The ecology of email use recounted in these stories shows the limitations of the platform in team-based office cultures. The move to To: after the failure of CC: is a symptom of the urgency felt by workers unable to prioritize tasks or afford the time to project empathy for their co-workers' different priorities and schedules. This is especially the case with growing numbers of workers only ever encountered as a virtual, online presence. Technology exacerbates team-members' different attitudes to tasks, arising from the different duties they perform, all of which creates a layer of additional communication that has to be registered and managed. In the context of complicated bureaucratic organizations, what begins as a democratic communication platform just as often becomes an opportunity for co-workers to force their own agendas on to others' schedules, obstructing individuals' capacity to manage their workload.

Perhaps it was her sensitivity to CC: protocol that made Miranda remember the following anecdote, one of few examples that any of the study's participants could recall where email policies had been openly mentioned in the office:

> The only place I've seen anything in writing around the company is on the toilet doors in the Melbourne office. On the back of the toilet doors in the Melbourne office they have this poster about being a "Super Emailer." And it has a guideline for when to use email. So, "Do you CC in people if they need to be aware of the issue but there's no action? That's when you CC. You include people in the email in the To if it's an issue they need to know about it plus there's an action for them." So it goes through all these guidelines . . . "If you're going to do a Reply All do these people all need to know about it or is just for the individual?" It's actually good. I like it. But it's the only place I've seen it – on the back of the toilet door in the Melbourne office. It looks like management made it, maybe a while ago. It's brilliant. I love it. You sit there and go, "Hmmm, yes that last email I sent, did everybody need to know about it?"

In this example, the register of teamwork underwrites the appeal to workers to consider others before sending email. The pedagogical intent of the poster is heightened by its location in the most personal of locations. The intimacy of work here takes crude form, as management considerations invade one of the few spaces of reprieve from the job.[6] If having such a poster in the toilet seemed symbolic of the way this employer considered its employees should be making use of company time, the story also helps reinforce how responsible email use is something the worker alone must navigate, with the interests of the team always in mind.

Rising above it

Workers in the study who could protect themselves from teamwork's coercive dimensions were typically in senior roles. These workers could choose to ignore ongoing email conversations until they had played themselves out. Directors also had assistants dedicated to managing email. At this level, managers spoke with disdain at some of their subordinates' use of "carbon copy." This was particularly the case when feuding colleagues deliberately copied directors into discussions to accelerate power plays and bring conflicts to a head. In these instances, heads of organizations like Barbara would take swift action to resolve matters in person, conscious of the paper trail that email created. (For those in Australian government jobs, freedom of information legislation makes email the equivalent of a public document.)

Typically, those in senior roles also spent far more time in meetings, whether with clients or developing workplace policy, which further affected their capacity to read email. Workers lower down the hierarchy were the ones sitting at their desks monitoring messages on arrival, and in this way email was something of a barometer of the highs and lows of the day. Georgia, one of the library's Directors, explained these different dynamics succinctly:

> I find some of the emails frustrating in that it's so easy for people to send you emails and then expect a response [. . .] What else I have to do in a day, I couldn't respond to all my emails so I feel a bit frustrated that I can't always respond [. . .] It could be a staff member further down the organization sends me an email and it could be an important issue to them but in the scheme of things . . . and I don't respond, so I guess I do feel a bit guilty that I don't deal with that in the time frame that they want.

Following the directives of the IT committee Georgia herself served on, Jenny had been charged with the task of developing "email efficiencies" in the library's business plan. Recall from previous chapters that Jenny regarded email use as the way she presented herself "as a professional." When interviewed, Jenny appeared worried about the job assigned to her because "the last thing I want to do is send out another email telling people how to manage their email." To her reckoning, "these days it's quite acceptable to have a whole lot of emails in your inbox," but she also thought, "there are still some people who are clinging to this idea that unless you clean your inbox out all the time there's something wrong with the work or the email or how many are being sent." Jenny claimed that she'd "become more and more comfortable with more and more emails sitting in my inbox as the years go by" – suggesting she had reached a point of transcendence in dealing with the deluge. In the same conversation, Jenny admitted that she found it hard to concentrate on her work during office hours: "my thinking sometimes can get a bit more flitty at work when I'm interrupted regularly. I start doing 15 minutes on something instead of just working solidly." For Jenny, one of the benefits of being at home to work was the possibility of "uninterrupted work time . . . I just do the work. Whereas I wouldn't not have my inbox open at work." In this way, Jenny embodied the contradictions of her colleagues in having "a commitment" to having her email open even though it was "a distraction" from her job. The culture of teamwork meant that turning off email "would be like taking the phone off the hook" during a typical day. The comparison to the phone is telling, since Jenny explained:

> people use email like a quick phone call used to be. You can just shoot those quick answers off. I think the reason I then feel committed to keeping it open is because it lets people get on with their work if they get that quick answer from me and they can keep going. I know I can feel frustrated if I just want a quick answer from someone and I ask them via email, why they don't get back to me and then I can progress it. I think it's probably how I feel about how I would like other people to behave.

Chapter 7 will explore some of the contradictions in Jenny's approach to email further. For the moment, what's instructive about her conception of online availability is that it is how she lets it be known that she is a good team-player. Email is the way Jenny helps other people "get on with their work," even though it is also the obstacle to getting her own work done.

In contrast to the teamwork culture of the library, an IT specialist for the broadcaster had found software solutions to the problem of email overload in his team. Frank's colleagues were spread across different cities and states – "as far west as Geraldton and as far north as Cairns and as far south as Hobart." He used a range of options including messenger clients and mobile phone text to make contact across several time zones. As he explained:

> we found that we were having a lot of conversations that were one line emails that were going backwards and forwards. So then we started using Google Talk because we can; the windows will just pop up and you can see if people are there and that sort of thing. Then

[you] just have those one line conversations there, without your email being piled up with 20 emails all with one line answers and responses.

While a number of organizations in the study had tried to institute messenger programs, they never took hold, mainly due to a lack of training and habit. By contrast, as one of the key technology experts in the organization, Frank's heightened awareness of new programs and devices matched his seniority as leader of his team. He was therefore able to decide which technologies would be used, and make sure staff were adequately trained to use them. It was this combination of knowledge *and* power that translated to notably convivial and efficient communication with colleagues.

Lingering connections

The significance of "team leaders" in securing the practices and energies of employees is worth further consideration in any discussion of contemporary office culture. In this study, telco workers showed particular affection for their leader, Holly, whose enthusiasm was clearly inspiring for those in the marketing team. As a major restructure in the company brought on a raft of redundancies, however, Holly was one of the many telco employees who faced a severance payout and termination of her role during the period of research. To an outsider, the wisdom of this decision was unfathomable, since it was Holly who had elicited the hyper-productivity evident in Claire and Miranda, among others. Having successfully orchestrated an effective team to the benefit of her employer, Holly was shown the door like anyone else as the financial crisis took hold. In this way she joined the fate of other middle managers of the past decade who, "charged with the task of 'making meaning', communicating management initiatives to baffled employees, and passing on bad news about redundancies," were also among "the most likely employees to be sacked." The "relative expense and expendability" of middle management is now the precarious fate of the successful (Moran, 2005: 44).

If the retrenchments shattered any belief in the company slogan of "people power," former team-members at the telco stayed in touch in the months afterwards, using online platforms. "Technology has been keeping me up to date with everyone," Jodi said in early 2009. "That's how we get together. We all caught up last Friday night, about 12 of us who were made redundant . . . We all had drinks and that's how we had the event; we invited people on

Facebook." Miranda, one of the few original team-members to survive the restructure, also used technology in this way. Her new colleagues in pricing weren't as interested in communicating for fun: "they're not marketers so they're not as chatty. They're very heads down, numbers driven. It's just that mindset. You contact people if you want to ask a specific question about a particular issue and that's over the phone and email." Miranda used chat software on days she worked from home to contact the "old team" dispersed throughout the office and beyond. Chat was less about work and "more of a social how you going, I'm not there, what's happening in the office kind of thing . . . [if] I'm working from home or away I'll use it to contact my old team back here or for personal [reasons]. That's how I use it now." Miranda wasn't a Facebook user at the time the study began, but she joined eventually to keep in the loop with news from old colleagues. Photos of well-deserved holidays, newborn babies, and job adventures overseas cemented bonds that had been formed entirely through the workplace and the team.

Miranda and Jodi's use of social media clearly shows a desire to stay in touch with the team despite the group's actual disintegration. Social media are a means to cope with the loss of close colleagues, when work is no longer the shared context for daily intimacies. This continued socializing with colleagues dispersed from the original office context is therefore testimony to the solidarities that developed during their time as co-workers. To some extent, the team *did* grant them a sense of community, "bearing witness to each other's lives." As the next chapter will elaborate further, Facebook provides a vital source of information as employees navigate the uncertainties of non-continuing work. It is the constant means of communication for those still employed as much as for those newly retrenched searching for jobs.

Without her foundational encounter with a set of physically present co-workers, Miranda's new position in the telco may have proven far more isolating. As the sole representative for her section of the company that was based in Brisbane, she shared the fate of Richard, the foreign correspondent from chapter 2, and Sam, the arts journalist in chapter 3. Their experiences are only likely to become more common as workplaces look to manage the decline in face-to-face interaction with virtual work environments.[7] But as this chapter has shown, there are still benefits to be found in sharing office space with others in spite of the coercive dimensions to team-work culture. A workplace free of *any* face-to-face office collegiality presents its own kinds of neuroses.[8] The logic of teamwork is part of a wider set of changes to the workplace designed to dissolve hierarchies and make the office appear friendly and fun (*The Economist* 2010). But, for many, these orchestrated friendships engineered by specifically hired experts come at the expense of more spontaneous forms of social contact. This was certainly the feeling of older employees in the study who remembered the pleasures of sharing regular breaks and free time with colleagues. Clive saw email as one of the key factors contributing to a general intensification of work:

> I think that's what's generating a lot of the environmental stress around the place. When I first started teaching in a university, there were high pressure moments, at the beginning of the term or the semester, and as you got to exam time, and things like that . . . but in between you'd have a six-week holiday period which was reasonably your own time to organize. And even in term there were opportunities that you could go and just have coffee with the students and things like that. All of that kind of laidback environment in the university, I think that's completely gone. And I think to the detriment of the university really . . . Where I started off a lot of my teaching, the whole university – the teaching staff would all gather in the senior common room at 10.30 for coffee and tea, and at 3.30 in the afternoon you'd take at least half an hour if not three quarters of an hour out just to catch up with colleagues and have some tea. Well, nobody does that round the university any more. It'd be considered profligate or something.

In accordance with Clive's reflection, heavily committed students and busy parents in the study felt pressure to make the most of their time at work, eating lunch at their desk, or avoiding lunch altogether if it meant leaving on time. The pace of the office environment gave employees the sense that they had no time for unproductive conversations. This context explains the present situation in which demonstrations of workplace unity and friendliness are forced to become part of the working day through birthday morning teas, Friday afternoon drinks and weekend get-to-know-you retreats. These social dimensions press upon workers the need to remain convivial in their jobs and talk to each other in emulation of the spontaneous community that now apparently eludes them. In previous experiences of office culture, the tea room or the cigarette break may have provided the basis for more regular opportunities for collegial interaction. Here, the latent effects of workplace health-and-safety policies are perhaps yet to be fully acknowledged.[9] At today's hotdesks, a perpetual time crunch combines with the surveillance potential of email to push the more affable exchanges of office life elsewhere.

And more often than not we find this other space to be online. G-Talk, MSN, Twitter, and blogs are the flipside to the coercive intimacy of the modern workplace as much as they are an escape from it. The next chapter explains how these platforms are testimony to the atomization many employees experience at work and the persistent desire to create intimate connections in spite of such conditions.

Meanwhile, this chapter has shown that the social bonds developed between co-workers in the office are a contributing factor in extending work hours. Loyalty to the team has the effect of making extra work seem courteous and common sense, which is particularly problematic for poorly compensated part-time workers. The "team" is an accommodating signifier. It helps to express engagement and commitment when loyalties lie not with the organization or even necessarily the job, but with the close colleagues who are the main point of daily interaction. It is the inevitable link between teamwork and email culture in modern office culture that makes this so complicated. Email encourages exercises in professional projection, since it is one of few ways employees regularly inhabit their colleagues' day-to-day consciousness. Email's storage capacity also encourages the presumption that writing a message will avoid unnecessary interruptions and enhance colleagues' productivity – especially when this is seen as an unequivocal good. "I suppose we do it because of speed or something," Clive reflected. "If you send an email, you're not getting involved in conversation." What may be forgotten in this transaction is that the speed that is assumed in sending an email message really only works one way. Email ultimately reaches a destination, namely, the inbox of fellow employees who rarely have time to handle its contents with care. The irony of the information and communication revolution is this vast volume of email that amasses between corridors and across floors, over business parks and campuses each day, and how this appears to be the leading means by which verbal communication between co-workers has been neutralized.

A sense of obligation to the team suits middle-class tendencies to want to please others and maintain cordial appearances. As a horizon for social ethics, however, it leaves much to be desired. Ultimately teamwork narrows workers' concerns to a set of objectives that fit the requirements for competitive advantage and commercial profit. This is what the euphemistic plaques in the arrivals foyer of workplaces only serve to remind us. A worrying myopia is apparent in the schedules of employees in this chapter who cathect their passions to the priorities of the organization while the concerns of the outside world are kept far from view. Team-based logic is a leading example of the way "office life reproduces itself not so much through ideological indoctrination as through daily routines that come to seem inexorable and unchangeable" (Moran 2005: 31). For organizations seeking to mobilize the loyalties of mobile workers, teamwork's benefits are ideological and financial. Positive connotations of a democratic workplace free from hierarchy or exploitation advance a wider business agenda to manipulate feelings of friendship built among workers. Email has been a formidable means to achieve these aims in workplaces of the past decade. A further stage in the process is the topic of the next chapter.

5

Facebook Friends

Security Blankets and Career Mobility

If each generation has its age-defining moment, in years to come 2008 will perhaps be remembered as the summer of Facebook. Over the course of this project, one social networking platform captured the interest of study participants and the wider public alike. In Australia, as in many anglophone countries, Facebook moved swiftly from a status of source of public panic – a cause célèbre for "old" media exploiting parental concerns about strangers in the house (Baxter 2008) – to an eventual degree of mundanity as companies and households each came to terms with its potential opportunities and threats. Building on the business-based marketing for mobile devices discussed in chapter 1, which suited the priorities of a frequent flyer clientele, Facebook's massive uptake created the impetus for a range of advertising campaigns targeting a wider constituency. Teens and students were addressed by a range of images showing happening youth accessing "Facebook on the go," particularly by means of the "smartphones" emerging from Nokia, BlackBerry, and Apple. A notable Telstra advertisement from 2009 warned: "If you've got time to Facebook, you've got time to call your mum." The nation's largest telco seemed obliged to remind young people of the need to check in with parents, such were the immersive temptations of cruising updates and profiles. The ad's moralizing tone was a notable instance of business attempts to set the terms for appropriate etiquette in the face of new technology.[1] The Facebook reference addressed the tension apparently playing out in families across the nation, as compulsive checking of online media appeared poised to threaten established forms of family connection and intimacy.

What the campaign failed to appreciate was that mothers were also joining Facebook during the same period with the distinct intention of keeping in touch with their children. Online social networking was routinely depicted in the media as the terrain of the young, single, and carefree, suggesting that households were generationally divided in their enjoyment of this new communication platform (Driscoll and Gregg 2008a). As the demographic make-up for the website became clear, however, it was employers' desires to avoid time-wasting in the office that offered the most viable front for public concern (Jenkins 2008). The success with which organizations developed an effective "social media strategy" – to keep employees content and harness the power of Web 2.0 technologies for profit – became a new gauge of credibility that "Generation Y" job-seekers could add to their list of requirements.

Facebook stands as the iconic application for the period this book documents. This is particularly in comparison to its main rival in English-speaking territories, MySpace, which catered to a younger audience, one more explicitly gathered around music promotion and other strands of the night-time economy.[2] While Twitter also gained market share during the course of the study, Facebook's popularity amongst a mainstream, middle-class, office-dwelling user base best illustrates the seamless combination of professional and personal identity that is at stake in the shift to intimate work, where "contact" equals "friend." Amassing these relationships in a unique biographical configuration, Facebook's rise to prominence reflects the significance of work in the lives of white-collar professionals. It highlights work's central influence on status and esteem on a daily basis, just as it demonstrates work's capacity to generate intimate relationships and pleasures to withstand these quotidian affects. Through "status updates," "posted items," "pokes," and "gifts" (the latter often specific to one's profession), Facebook users showcase their interests and obsessions to a cast of sympathetic onlookers. If Larry Grossberg described the mainstream appeal of rock music as "a way of making it through the day" (1997: 115), for deskbound employees, Facebook provides a similarly reliable solace, especially when long hours prevent other kinds of connection.

At a time of increased social mobility, this chapter describes Facebook as the "security blanket" for workers conscious of the need to remain flexible, available, and likable in a dynamic employment market. Facebook makes bearable all of the potentially overwhelming encounters of life online and on the job, as friends and family can be brought along as virtual company through a succession of non-continuing projects and positions. At the same time, social networking sites allow mobile individuals the benefits of a new form of prospective labor increasingly vital for survival in a reputation-based employment market (Solove 2007). A Facebook profile and a set of contacts provides an ongoing character-based CV for workers to draw upon to withstand the instability of "flexible" careers. In this way, online communities serve as a grounding mechanism and reassuring presence that in the past may have been provided by more geographically proximate others. When work takes people away from an original foundational community, Facebook friends provide the continuity often missing in the "liquid lives" (Bauman 2005; Deuze 2007) that result from job-related "churn" (Delaney 2009) and "drift" (Sennett 1998). Across cities and countries, social networking sites have fast become the principal means by which upwardly mobile workers cushion the impact of unfamiliar surroundings. Online connections assist in the most ordinary day-to-day issues posed by a life of transitory home-making, from finding a flatmate to finding a doctor, getting a haircut to getting a couch.

Facebook offers a reliable locus for affection for the growing number of workers for whom traditional forms of community seem lacking. Comment sections, wall space, email and instant messaging are just some of the ways it incites convivial discourse that rivals the tonelessness of other communication platforms like email (see chapter 4). Add-on applications allow gestures and mementos to accrue over time, acting as tangible evidence of friends' ongoing presence – not to mention the prospect of further "hook-ups" in future. It is this potential, and the constant and reassuring guarantee of presence, that is Facebook's permanent consolation. Unlike the mass appeal of rock music, however, Facebook's popularity is highest among a particular subset of the knowledge class. Susceptibility to Facebook relies on the possession of a set of mutually shared dispositions – a similar "habitus" (Bourdieu 1984) – the most prominent of which is regular and prolonged Internet use. Rules of participation and membership separate the casual Facebook user from the larger community conversation. Even if there are different ways of using the site, structural constraints imposed by design innovations hamper efforts to veer from what are established as normative displays of affection and disaffection. Like all social networking platforms, Facebook relies on an intricate combination of performance cues that are central to effective use and optimal enjoyment.

The first of these is a certain comfort with sharing relatively personal information in a comparatively public space that may be subject to outside manipulation. This "broadcast impulse" is the willingness to engage in personal displays voluntarily, in spite of the possibility that others can make use of such revelations for unknown purposes. As the YouTube slogan put it, to "broadcast yourself" on social networking sites is to recognize that what matters to oneself is at least as significant as any prospective engagement with others.[3] Facebook's interpellative address – "What are you doing, right now?" and the more recent, "What's on your mind?" – invites the user to share even the most minor thought or activity, and to believe that doing so is significant. Those accustomed to a more traditional broadcast model for entertainment, having been brought up on a diet of radio and television, for instance, find this the most disturbing aspect of social networking sites. But one of the easiest ways to explain the "new" of new media is this shifting recognition that messages no longer need to be limited or deemed worthy of broadcast by others. This is also the threat that "new" media prove to professional identities premised on expertise in refining and disseminating information (a fact that is hardly incidental to this study's focus on journalists, librarians, and academics). In the context of trends discussed in this book already, however, there is a further reason why Facebook's apparently "trivial" snippets of information prove interesting to an audience only slightly connected to each other. This is because structural developments in the workplace may in fact prevent the likelihood of more significant, long-term connections beyond the computer screen.

The logic of likes

The work of sociologist Pierre Bourdieu offers an astute register for understanding how online social networks attract and favor similar types. While they invite spontaneity, Facebook updates fit the "scriptural economy" (de Certeau 1988) of middle-class literacy in that the power to manipulate the written word is used with care. On social networking platforms, users craft their self-image through a process of fabulation (Crawford 2009). The broadcast dimension of status updates brings with it the expectation that the image projected is a favorable one. To the extent that the individual focus of Facebook creates community, this is largely attributable to the logic of like attracts like. As Bourdieu explained this tendency of "elective affinities":

> Those whom we find to our taste put into their practices a taste which does not differ from the taste we put into operation in perceiving

their practices. Two people can give each other no better proof of the affinity of their tastes than the taste they have for each other. (Bourdieu 1984: 243)[4]

The Facebook page is a marker of taste in that "it unites all those who are the product of similar conditions distinguishing them from all others. And it distinguishes in an essential way, since taste is the basis of all that one has – people and things – and all that one is for others, whereby one classifies oneself and is classified by others" (Bourdieu 1984: 56). A key aspect of Facebook's appeal is to provide recommendations about useful or interesting information based on the security gleaned from personal networks. This recommendation process, of course, also extends to people, and the exclusive feeling of discovery that transpires when mutual recognition of shared taste leads to the "serendipity" of connecting with further, previously unknown, like-minded others.

It is both an addition and an endorsement to be allowed to join someone's Facebook community. This entrepreneurial dimension to friending practices was captured early on in the phrase "Thanks for the add": the ritual acknowledgment shared by MySpace users when someone "adds" you to their list of friends. Both MySpace and Facebook pivot on the invitation to display and market a coherent self that can be assessed and consumed by others (Hearn 2008). Due to the taste logic of these sites, the benefit that is recognized is that friendship allows one's own profile to be circulated for free to "a wider market of strangers" (Mills, 1973: 251).

It is in the very nature and structure of the profile page that social networking sites reveal their role as a marker of class position. The profile page invites us to create a succession of distinctions that define our identity against others. These distinctions nonetheless communicate that we belong to a particular group. In Bourdieu's terms, cultural capital arises in the combination of disposition and entitlement that provides the confidence in displaying our preferences to an audience. Entering tastes and favorite things to construct a profile page provides a readily available repository for others to appreciate our own distinguishing features.[5] But, beyond these gestures, users also demonstrate preferences explicitly by voting in polls, taking personality quizzes or simply clicking "I like" after a friend does something interesting or amusing online. Facebook fosters a "cultivated disposition" in Bourdieu's sense by naturalizing the arbitrary tastes and choices of a specific demographic. Taste is acquired not only "by moving in a universe of familiar, intimate objects" that the site provides, but also by developing "a relation of immediate familiarity with the things of taste" (Bourdieu 1984: 77) through the sharing of gifts, links, and preferences. Facebook's homophillic tendencies are also shown in the forms of humor rewarded and encouraged by the site. A particularly instructive example of this in the course of writing this book was an application called Bogan Gifts. In Australia, a "bogan" is an affectionate term for working-class, suburban dwellers with modest aspirations and simple tastes (much like the English expression "chav"). The premise of the Bogan Gifts application was to allow users to send presents or tokens to each other that were both iconic of bogan stereotypes but often familiar objects from childhood.

The premise of the application is like many others on Facebook. The sharing of objects, humorous precisely because of their status as the opposite of taste, is a way of expressing affection and affiliation between friends. But Bogan Gifts is more helpful than most in terms of demonstrating Bourdieu's claim that for those adapting to a middle class lifestyle:

> the "horrors" of popular kitsch are easier to "recuperate" than those of petit-bourgeois imitation, just as the "abomination" of bourgeois taste can begin to be found "amusing" when they are sufficiently dated to cease to be "compromising". (Bourdieu 1984: 62)

Figure 5.1 Selection from "Bogan Gifts" Facebook application

Class mobility is central to Bogan Gifts' appeal and success. The program operates on the pleasurable relief that opportunity has intervened to place users at some distance from the "horrors" of childhood objects. This regular reflection of the "abominations" of taste provides a stage for friends to express their relative distance from previously compromising elements of an inherited lifestyle. Games provide an outlet for discussing the similar class background that individuals have been able to escape through educational and employment mobility. The rehabilitation of such objects in this new space therefore becomes a further badge of membership, familiarity, and humor, although there is poignancy at play. The self-reflexivity Bogan Gifts summons from users regarding the relationship between present and past recalls the feeling of displacement that, in another context, Richard Hoggart (1957) described as the melancholic fate of the Scholarship Boy (see Gregg 2006: chapter 2).

Bogan Gifts is just one of a number of examples that reveal Facebook's popularity with a particular demographic at a time when class mobility is commonplace, if not also a rational expectation. Facebook and its many applications and quizzes provide an encompassing venue to play out the anxieties of the beneficiaries of cultural capital and career progression. While not all users come to such applications with similar experiences, Facebook's wider mandate to connect similar types makes it a venue for users with a shared habitus. As the following sections will highlight, Bourdieu's writing is a helpful reminder that "the principle of the pleasure derived from these refined games for refined players lies, in the last analysis, in the denied experience of a social relationship of membership and exclusion" (Bourdieu 1984: 499).

Facebook intimacy

Another of Facebook's consolations therefore is that it promises to be immersive. This is the basis of its appeal for users with the relative freedom to have the platform running throughout the day and into the night. It also explains the resolve expressed by many in this study who were bent on avoiding Facebook's time-consuming properties. Engagement with the site must be performed in ritualistic ways to signify interest in and reciprocity with others, otherwise the experience as a whole risks being voyeuristic. In the context of workloads already discussed in the book so far, such expectations appeared to many as just another online obligation.

The pressure to respond to friend requests was mentioned by Peter, a 57-year-old university lecturer. He felt "restricted" in his use of the site because his name was so recognizable to students. His measured approach to the site was to "try not to let it run ahead of me . . . Work is for the soul, but not beyond a certain point." Others opted out of Facebook due to a similar lack of time. Tony, an Associate Professor of Education, knew the site was popular with his kids and students, but didn't use Facebook himself: "I just feel that everything I do – to do another thing would be just too much." Despite these hesitations, particularly among older workers, the number of people using Facebook in the study increased over time. While some participants had stopped using it before we met, no one using it at the start of the study had stopped, and several who had claimed its irrelevance in initial interviews were regular users later. Clive, a university professor in charge of a research center, was one of the growing number of Facebook enthusiasts: "I resisted getting on Facebook for a long time, but then I got on and I can see how infectious it is. It's true." One of the pleasures he appreciated was being able to see another side to the colleagues usually encountered in serious, professional settings. For instance, one high-powered diplomatic official he was friends with showed a particular fondness for Scrabulous, and this was something he enjoyed seeing. He also noticed that other friends spent a lot of effort "demonstrating how engaged they are with all of the big issues all of the time," and was worried that he might be seen to do the same: "People realize I've been reading *Liquid Fear* by Zygmunt Bauman for about two weeks now."

Clive considered Facebook "a leisure thing" and "a break from the normal routine." He felt "uncomfortable using Facebook at work." The significance of the site was that: "All of my colleagues on Facebook, who are indeed work colleagues, will now see that at certain times of the day I'm prepared to be frivolous and non-serious and will take the film test and things like that with everybody else." These distinctions were important even though they were not necessarily shared by all users. For Clive, this came to prominence when a colleague "caught him out" using Facebook rather than responding to a work request. The person wrote to say, "I see that you scored 79 per cent on your Disney test, what about my proposal?" For Clive, this was "an interesting jumbling of the private and public" where he was reprimanded "for being frivolous."

As an expert in international affairs, active in both NGO and scholarly settings, Clive recognized more than most the difference between Facebook's trivial and serious potential. His global connections made him "more and more persuaded" that social networking sites can "become powerful means of influence." Clive's comments are an interesting indication of the potential for new media to expand the audience for political issues alongside traditional readerships for academic ideas. In the wake of social networking technologies, he told us:

> if I wanted to put something serious in an area where I think it would be read by a lot of people, I wouldn't necessarily go straight to a journal. I might actually contemplate putting a sign on my Facebook . . . saying I've just got this information, you might want to follow it up. If you look at my Facebook, you'll see that the second secretary of the New Zealand High Commission was giving me updated briefings on what was happening in the Solomons. So, somewhat trivial technologies are actually becoming quite serious.

In other professions, such as journalism, Facebook was also used to enhance the possibilities for communication that were already a part of the job. In his role as assistant producer for the breakfast program, Patrick would often check the news circulating amongst his network of friends to get a sense of the popular issues of the day and to have something to offer as a story idea. The presence indicators in Facebook's chat function were another way journalists used the site to organize stories to deadline. As the following chapter illustrates, these work-based applications for online social networking were a mundane dimension of the job in industries focused on engaging with the public. But, as Patrick discovered, using Facebook for work raised problems in terms of balancing a professional identity alongside the more relaxed persona he sought to enjoy by using the site.

Patrick's "creative" lifestyle directly contributed to these problems. Not only did he use Facebook for his radio job, but increasingly it was part of his work as a practicing musician. Navigating the changing audiences for MySpace and Facebook as he tried to promote his live performances made his use of technology seem at times overwhelming:

> I feel as though I need to be using it. If it weren't for music, to be quite honest, I think I would be a lot more judicious and harsh with my use of technology at home. Obviously I want to be in touch with people, but I feel as though technology is blackmailing me. I'm feeling as though if I don't maintain some kind of – especially with music – online hyperactive presence, not that I aspire to this but just my impressions, that suddenly everything that's dear in my life would

just sort of go away and disappear and vanish, that I will have no friends, that no one will turn up to my gigs and then I will practically cease to exist. I mean, that's kind of the reality, that's the threat that I feel with technology at the moment. It's a terrible thing.

Patrick's feelings of "blackmail" paint a clear picture of the coercive bind implicit in online networking. Facebook is a kind of "compulsory friendship" (Gregg 2007) through which Patrick maintains perceptions of his own likability and popularity via an ongoing "hyperactive presence." In creative professions, this entrepreneurial dimension to online platforms that allows users to generate a fan base for their work is a legacy of the patterns of interaction earlier established on MySpace. The music-oriented demographic for this site developed an effective ecology of support and sustenance for emerging independent talent that has become the basis for considerable economic modeling and speculation (Benkler 2006; Anderson 2004). With the mainstream uptake of Facebook, however, a widening audience for self-broadcasting poses a new kind of conflict. Users never quite know whether they are performing their endearing personality as an end in itself or for the purposes of profit:

> Facebook for me was I liked the idea of having something that had nothing to do with music, because MySpace for me is to do with music. So I like the idea of my Facebook profile being non-music orientated. I've since noticed, and I've kind of been taken against my will, that people have been abandoning MySpace and now Facebook is increasingly for bands and solo artists and [is also] music orientated. So now I've just kind of had to accept my fate that I have nowhere to hide, that my music will fucking just invade every single part of my life and I have no private life except the face-to-face interactions in real life.[6]

Patrick's perception of being "taken against my will" and "accepting my fate" are further indications of Facebook's coercive intimacy. He sees little choice but to adapt his preferences to suit the dominant uptake of the site, noting that his opportunities for privacy and relaxation appear to be dwindling. The additional complication in Patrick's use of Facebook was that he also considered it the place where he could escape the feeling of pressure to perform his professional persona with the broadcaster, his "day job." He knew, for instance, that the broadcaster had its own group on Facebook, but claimed: "I just don't know why you would want to join it." On the whole, he chose not to become Facebook friends with people from the radio station "unless they're actually genuine friends."

> Everyone else who is just an acquaintance or a colleague at work . . . I haven't befriended because I can't think of anything worse than them kind of being in every part of my life and commenting on my fucking status. I think I would just keel over. I can't bear that thought.

The network of friends Patrick has developed on Facebook is presented here as something valuable that is worth protecting. His resistance to being exposed to the scrutiny of work colleagues shows the function of this online community as a place of respite from the expectations of his job. The multiple identities Patrick occupies in using Facebook for different purposes gives an insight into the processes of differentiation that matter in accepting the terms of friendship. His experience complicates any simplistic reading of the site's manifold functions, just as it highlights the particular constraints and opportunities of the platform for adult users and professionals.[7]

Other young workers in the study also pursued complex patterns of management and control in juggling their online and professional identities. Angela used Facebook "for social emailing," to keep a distinction between work and personal life. She used Facebook as a safe space for chat during the workday, one that was protected from the surveillance of formal email, and had the advantage of being available in her multiple workplaces. In Sam's case too:

> I try to have some degree of separation because there's a lot of personal stuff up there and because I'm a queer and so I go to queer radical sex events that are often stuff that I wouldn't necessarily show my workmates.

Sam considered her work colleagues to be friends "in real life," but online the case was different: "I certainly wouldn't actively seek out a connection with any of my work colleagues," The "one or two" she had connected with were justified because "I know them well enough that they know me anyway [and] it's not going to be anything shocking for them." Sam's perspective is interesting for the way that it places thoughts of others at the heart of her friending practice. She protects her workmates from exposure to her outside-work persona to save the embarrassment of others being offended.

It is hardly incidental that Sam and Patrick appeared the most articulate in describing their use of Facebook. The importance of an ongoing group of friends online bears direct relation to the fluctuating conditions of their paid work. As "creatives" employed in precarious positions, Sam and Patrick recognized that their bases for loyalty needed to reside elsewhere than the workplace. Their use of

Facebook showed an awareness of the need to be prepared for unknown eventualities. While each maintained their profiles as opportunities to relax and communicate with friends, it's also clear that these small pleasures involved an intricate set of negotiations to audit their identity and present their lives in particular ways. By the end of 2009, as reports emerged that employers were asking for print-outs of Facebook profiles before shortlisting for jobs, these modulations of self-image were only fitting. Those who had failed to learn the lesson of online self-management were facing the consequences.[8]

Friends in need

Facebook friends are an index of the changing stakes involved in the shift to flexible work and contract careers. The selective use of Facebook for work purposes indicates that users exercise a degree of agency in allowing access to their "network capital." As Bradwell and Reeves (2008: 21) describe this term:

> Being part of an organization is still hugely important for our sense of identity and how others judge our value, status and potential. But the role of *network* capital is increasing, and the influence of personal reputation, history and network presence will be vital.

For workers like Sam and Patrick, network capital provides opportunities beyond the limits of the specific organizations that employ them. But it also brings the burden of managing their own "network reputation." The labor of friendship includes deciding who will be given access to the benefits of connection in addition to the performance of a vigilant and "hyperactive" presence for those selected. For employers, the dilemma posed by this new form of reputation management is that if an individual leaves an organization, "they take their network capital with them," even when this set of relationships has been developed and maintained on company time. While the interviews documented in this study at least question whether this is pragmatically the case (salaried employees had little work time to waste on Facebook, and tended to use it outside the office), the wider point remains. Organizations now face the problem of how to summon loyalty from workers when their individual reputations are rarely secured through ongoing identification with the firm. In this new culture, online networking is key to both work and personal gain (Bradwell and Reeves 2008: 65).

To date, employers' efforts to capitalize on the network capital of employees have fluctuated between opportunism and punishment, in an attempt to minimize the threat Facebook poses to productivity and brand reputation (Moses 2009). Either response misrecognizes the site's current function in the white-collar workplace. In the context of office cultures that require conviviality and teamwork in all online dealings, Facebook acts as the necessary safety valve for workers needing a place to vent the many negative affects accompanying office life. Social networking sites are a psychological buffer zone for a work experience that offers few avenues for ordinary sociability off-screen (Morris 2009).

Drawing on the work of Erving Goffman's classic study, *The Presentation of Self in Everyday Life* (1959), much of the critical writing on Facebook to date has worried that the effort required to project a polished, public online image threatens the possibility of maintaining a "back region" of behavior – one that is, shall we say, "not fit for broadcast." In Goffman's theory, the "back region" is where we let our guard down, where friends accept us for who we really are, "behind the mask" of public appearances. The move to embrace online social media has been met with concerns that individuals are becoming accustomed to the "deep acting" (Hochschild and Machung 1989) of professional work; that they may no longer develop the skills to switch back to the "genuine" self once reserved for intimate others. Evidence presented in this chapter shows something slightly different. It is precisely the perception that Facebook friends *are* genuine that prompts employees to protect this online space from outside intrusions. It is the opportunity to engage in familiar exchanges with close friends during the workday that pushes many Facebook users online, since long hours at the office in many cases prevent the capacity to cultivate these friendships otherwise.

If "front region" behavior did become more predominant in leisure as well as labor time, this would constitute significant grounds for concern, since the emotional labor involved in maintaining professional appearances attracts such dubious recognition. This is why Bourdieu's theories are important to read in conjunction with Goffman's, to isolate the specific class demographic that these discussions favor. As Goffman acknowledged, those further up the class hierarchy have always spent more time in the front region, since doing so is a direct reflection of their higher status. "The higher one's place in the status pyramid," he wrote, "the smaller the number of persons with whom one can be familiar, the less time one spends backstage, and the more likely it is that one will be required to be polite as well as decorous" (Goffman 1973: 133).

Social networking sites are one of the ways class and power are reconfiguring to suit a new economic formation. Here, digital literacy takes on the character of enfranchisement, since Internet access is only the initial step in a wider circuit of cultural capital set up to reward those who are familiar and comfortable with being online. In the modern workplace, the performance of presence on Facebook profiles can even be said to be replacing the Fordist face as tantamount to the parameters for participation and survival.[9] The homophillic tendencies these platforms favor certainly make them significantly implicated in extending the present digital divide. Bourdieu's language of taste and affinity allows us to see how these activities relate to a longer history of cultural capital and the practices through which it is displayed and acknowledged.

Facebook's massive growth during the course of this study is best understood in the context of the increased class mobility that has come with broadening education opportunities and new forms of salaried work. These structural changes that accompanied the move to a flexible workplace required significant adjustments to service workers' needs for ongoing family and community support. The pleasures and anxieties that populate Facebook are the priorities of those who can take social mobility for granted. In this sense, it is important to note that the public friendships that Facebook makes possible aren't limited to the online era. For decades, the mobility involved in the pursuit of middle-class security and patronage has brought accompanying requirements in the domain of friendship. In *The Organization Man*, William H. Whyte spoke of the "outward personality" required of couples moving between company towns in the long march up the company ladder. The "web of friendship" he described in analyzing the social networks of dormitory suburbs in the United States is a precedent for the coercive friendships on the World Wide Web today. Whyte saw few alternatives to participation in the "outgoing life" of the neighborhood for couples seeking a sense of belonging in unfamiliar locations. His analysis highlights the enduring problem for professionals seeking to recapture a lost sense of community when work leads them away from home. It also offers an early indication of the limited avenues for intimacy available to busy professionals.

These first two chapters in the second part of the book show how online cultures provide a relatively safe space for workers to manage the demands of office life. Facebook friends and messaging buddies take on the role of collegial support when the workplace prevents such relationships from developing organically. Online friendships are the necessary recompense for a range of social and economic changes that include the intrusion of work into home and leisure space, the isolation of precarious employment, and the long-hours culture pursued by middle-class professionals. The extent to which people choose to conduct significant parts of their personal lives online, from finding the next book they should read to finding a life partner, says something about the opportunities for intimacy in a culture that is dominated by the schedules of office workers. It also questions the reliability of previous forms of social activity and affiliation in providing enduring and satisfying relationships.

At the same time, however, the particular benefits of online intimacy have been shown to accrue in the performance and appreciation of shared habits and tastes. The use of social networking sites is a means of affirming participation in an emerging class of globally mobile information workers. Facebook's mission to "connect people" pivots on the early Internet's novel promise to find ways of communicating with friends, as if no other medium had allowed this experience before. In doing so, it has consecrated a particular disposition or "habitus" assisting the class consolidation of the knowledge worker. Facebook's original location in the dorms of Harvard University should not be forgotten in assessing the site's mainstream uptake. Existing networks of privilege are reified in a very particular combination of textual performance, digital literacy, and useful contacts. Celebrating this in the language of serendipity and democratic progress, Facebook is the latest means by which the aspiring middle class creates distinctive expressions of its own privileged position in social space. This is because the command of virtual territories is increasingly crucial to the rewards to be won in society at large.[10]

In contrast to teamwork's ultimately narrow objective, to ensure efficiency and productivity for the organization, Facebook nonetheless makes us aware of a larger world, a wider community asking for our attention (Berlant 2007). Facebook opens workers' horizons beyond the daily concerns of the cubicle to keep them connected to other things that matter. To be sure, many of these outside concerns also affirm already established preferences and priorities, this being one of friendship's best qualities – to act as both conscience and consolation. But its performative nature and personal address is what makes Facebook synonymous with a new kind of presence, witnessing and responsibility within the otherwise anonymizing forces of global capital.

6

Know Your Product[1]

Online Branding and
the Evacuation of Friendship

In July 2009 the US electronics chain Best Buy placed an online job advertisement for the position of "Senior Manager: Emerging Media Marketing" at its head office in Richfield, Minnesota. Among the selection criteria was the requirement that the applicant have a minimum of 250 followers on the Internet platform Twitter. The successful candidate was needed to lead "Best Buy's mobile, social, and video marketing & media efforts to drive in-store and online sales, create sustainable word of mouth evangelists, and brand loyalists" (Banerjee 2009). By the time the story broke across international news outlets, the first job to be dependent on a quantitative measure of Twitter contacts had already been filled. Coming in the wake of the global economic downturn, the Best Buy story symbolized some of the changing opportunities for work available in a digitally connected era. Across a range of business and recruitment media in 2008–9, employees had been encouraged to join social networking sites in order to improve their prospects for security and success in challenging times. Here was proof that Tweeting was anything but trivial.

Growing in tandem with these developments, although with significantly less publicity, was a boom in new "career opportunities" for college interns interested in social media. Typically destined for marketing, communication, and journalism degrees, and often straight out of high school, students were hired for short-term, unpaid positions in summer breaks to investigate the viability of social media platforms for their employers. If 2008 was the summer of Facebook, it was also the summer that many young users spent much of their time working on the site for free to investigate its value for firms of all kinds. Sydney's Abacus Recruitment was one such company seeking to save money on salaries while staying abreast of exciting developments in online media. Marketing internships in "Social Networking Strategy" advertised in mid-2009 boasted a range of benefits – "Develop your marketing skills! Gain experience before you graduate! Flexible hours!" – for an unpaid role that required two days' work a week – only one of which included the privilege of an office (seek.com.au 2009). This book has already shown some of the pressures on casually employed white-collar apprentices to discount their labor to prove commitment and virtue (see chapter 3). Social marketing internships were the next step. Leaving school faced with a recession to rival any other, fresh-faced students were the main target for savvy businesses seeking to exploit the vulnerabilities produced by an unstable job market. Experience in temporary, unpaid positions was sold as the saving grace that would provide the competitive edge to withstand financial turmoil. The aura of new media hype and the popular fascination with Facebook combined with economic uncertainties to enshrine a whole new model of "sacrificial labor" (Ross 2004).

The uptake of social media for corporate ends was a natural extension of an already pervasive discourse in new economy literature inspired by Tom Peters' influential article "Brand You" (Peters 1998; Brady 2007). *Wired Magazine*'s elite readership was among the first to recognize the value of emerging technology platforms in promoting products and skills to new audiences. Web 2.0 evangelists hailed the Internet's unprecedented capacity to erase the hierarchies of an older era of business culture (see especially Shirky 2008; Bruns 2008). Meanwhile, PR fashions dictating the need to develop a "social networking strategy" were a major source of investment for organizations seeking to update their image, improve communication with clients, and enhance brand loyalty through emotional marketing (see Jenkins 2006).

In the celebratory strains of early adopters, many of whom found employment in expanded marketing departments, social media took the form of a second coming, a blessing for those true believers still recovering from the first dot.com boom and crash. A fresh crop of web prophets built careers trumpeting the benefits of participatory platforms for business application. Titles such as *Groundswell: Winning in a World Transformed by Social Technologies* (Li and Bernoff 2008); *Trust Agents: Using the Web to Build Influence, Improve Reputation, and Earn Trust* (Brogan and Smith, 2009);

Socialnomics: How Social Media Transforms the Way We Live and Do Business (Qualman 2009); and the crossover bestseller, *Here Comes Everybody: The Power of Organizing Without Organizations* (Shirky 2008) answered the big questions for busy executives, including how "Finding the Right 'Brand Voice' on Twitter" (Turner 2009) can avoid the lamentable fate of "Follow Fail" (Bartelby 2009).[2]

The mainstream uptake of key social networking sites MySpace and Facebook was often described during this period as powered by the leisure choices of the young. Countless studies investigated the nefarious practices of "self-branding" on broadcast platforms by teens and college students, with cautious and often moralizing conclusions. But it was the burgeoning PR industry, touting the commercial applications of online media that was equally central to these sites' growing dominance. The branding potential identified by business consultants provided a language that scholars appeared only willing to adopt to investigate online social networking practices that the previous chapter showed to be far more complex. In the words of Henry Jenkins, a key actor in the dialogues developing between big business and media scholarship, by the middle of the decade "entrenched institutions" were "reinventing themselves for an era of media convergence and collective intelligence" (2006: 24). New media technologies allowed consumers to "archive, annotate, appropriate, and recirculate media content in powerful new ways" (18), while media producers were able "to build stronger connections with their constituencies and consumers" (22). As scholars like Jenkins documented the empowering possibilities of these practices for media fans and audiences, consensus grew as to the positive benefits of cross-platform or "trans-media" production (Turner 2010).

In this process, little attention was paid to the experience of workers within and beyond the media industries that were the basis of convergence theory whose jobs were being fundamentally influenced by its assumptions.[3] In information jobs, employees were increasingly expected to multiply their labor across a growing number of media and communication outlets, in line with the preferences assumed of their target demographic. In public-sector as much as corporate settings, organizational commitments to public service added further weight to this expectation. In Jenkins's description, information and communication platforms were the "delivery technologies" for trans-media content that moved between producers on the one hand and consumers on the other. In this vision, the infrastructure of workers keeping these technologies running was considered incidental. Indeed, the use of delivery technologies for work as opposed to entertainment could not begin to be registered.

This chapter shows the effects of social media strategies on those actually providing the enhanced services that organizations were claiming as the winnings of the participatory revolution. In these workplaces, online obligations add to existing job descriptions without any previous job expectations being taken away, another instance of "function creep" in jobs dependent on communication technology. For creative professionals specifically employed to harness the youthful demographics assumed of new media platforms, bureaucratic workplaces often prevented the very means of access to online culture's participatory pleasures. In each case, organizations make strategic use of online culture for commercial purposes, and ask their employees to do the same. This entails a shift to colonize the very avenues for friendship and solidarity that previous chapters have described as the support structures for isolated working conditions. This section of the book therefore closes by asking a key question: if social media are one of the key means by which employees resist the intrusion of work on their personal lives, what kind of labor politics will be needed to resist management pressures to pilfer friendship networks for business benefit?

Participation's infrastructure

Time Magazine's move to enshrine You as person of the year at the end of 2006 was one of the first indications that social media would be a major focus for attention in the years captured by this study. The gesture was the ultimate manifestation of a wider cultural realization that the technologically equipped individual held new kinds of power in a participatory media environment. In workplaces across Brisbane, management efforts were everywhere moving to develop outward-facing initiatives to engage the public and interface with users across multiple media platforms. For employees, this new mandate often came at the expense of traditional job functions, as Patrick neatly explained:

> We are all – producers and presenters – expected to be uploading material to our website, to the point where we have been told that, if you need to drop an interview from your show to make time for uploading a story on the Internet, then so be it.

The new rule of thumb in Patrick's workplace was to prioritize online content. This marked a significant cultural shift for a broadcaster built on quality radio and television programming, and not

all employees were happy about it. Many wondered whether upload-
ing Internet content compromised a fundamental professional commitment "to make good radio." This was especially the case given
how blatantly management mandates emphasized the dispensa-
bility of individual stories – previously the bread and butter of the
working day.

One on-air presenter, Gary, had responded to the new management mandate with enthusiasm, and was "very, very active" upload-
ing material to the website, according to Patrick. Gary had developed
a system of writing blog posts from home when inspiration struck:
"he'll write five, ten blog posts in advance and time schedule them
to appear at intervals. You know, so if he's going away for a week,
you will still see blog posts . . . he's very, very diligent about that."
The opportunity to enhance audience interaction through online
contact was seen as a boon by Gary and other on-air personalities
with an established fan base. As another journalist for the network
suggested, using platforms like Twitter meant the network's well-
known identities "can actually have a personality" and express their
own opinions beyond specific stories.

Gary's willingness to maintain work obligations away from the
studio fit wider trends in the book so far that show the home space
expanding to accommodate additional work requests, particularly
among salaried workers. For Patrick, who was already struggling to
meet the demands of live to air broadcast in his allotted part-time
hours (see chapter 3), his colleague's commitment to online engagement was something of a relief. Producing additional content for the
website was one of the few ways Patrick was trying to place limits
on his workload.

During the study the broadcaster's drive to enhance online presence stretched to include blogging, online discussion, program
"guest books," transcripts, and podcasts as just some of the ways
audiences could participate in broadcast material. The Managing
Director strongly encouraged all on-air talent to use Twitter to
"meet modern audience demands for immediate, cross-platform
news" and maintain the network's formidable reputation (Scott
2010).[4] One journalist witnessing this transformation was Belinda,
a 30-year-old journalism graduate. At the start of the study she was
an opinion editor for the broadcaster's news website, where her role
was commissioning and coordinating short articles for blog publication. The tight turnarounds for online publishing involved a lot of
email, instant messaging, and phone calls with writers. She combined this with ongoing tasks such as monitoring comments on the
website and keeping up with the daily news cycle. In 2007, a year

which saw significant public interest in the Australian Federal
Election, Belinda was also charged with making sure the broadcaster
was compliant with legal obligations around election coverage by
avoiding defamatory publication. Here the participatory potential
of interactive platforms – the democratic affordances celebrated by
Web 2.0 prophets – created an obligation to maintain order in online
spaces, a task that paid little attention to office hours. Belinda had
noticed the network's blogging software was one of the few platforms able to be used beyond the strict firewalls of the broadcaster's
headquarters. As such, she felt the choice to use TypePad brought
"an unspoken expectation that you'll blog from home," which was
"not such a great thing for work–life balance I suppose."

Over time, Belinda's role changed to Acting Executive Producer
for the whole local news site, which brought a higher amount of
responsibility. By now she was coordinating schedules and training
new staff, as well as maintaining her own contributions to the
website through stories, blog posts, and Twitter. Her use of Twitter
was one way of understanding these changing expectations:

> At first I started off with an alias because I didn't really know what
> other people were doing and whether I should be – because I'm with
> [the broadcaster], should I be out there as myself? Then I decided to
> just change it to my name, so it's my name. But I'm still quite aware
> in the back of my mind that I have on my profile that I work for [the
> broadcaster]. So it's kind of a work-related thing. I don't Tweet a hell
> of a lot for personal stuff. And most of the people who follow me
> and the people that I follow are in the media. A group of colleagues,
> I suppose.

Belinda's use of Twitter develops from a position of curious exploration to professional adaptation as the norms of the platform begin
to take hold. Her experience shows a concern to weigh up questions
of personal privacy before ultimately giving way to the industry-
based conventions developed by others. In the course of this shift,
Belinda assesses the merits of differentiating between her personal
and professional identity in online space. Indeed, we could say that
her successful acculturation to the technology comes when she
reaches a point of synthesis between the two – a recognition this
book takes to be crucial for white-collar workers.

In her new role, Belinda was regularly "Tweeting" for the broadcaster's news feed – a combination of automatic Tweets that happened every hour, and "breaking news Tweets" that had to be shared
around the office. So while management stressed the need for
network personalities to use the platform to engage audiences,

Twitter was also being used behind the scenes to fulfill the broadcaster's established role as a news service. This new expectation was an addition to the work Belinda was already hired to perform, and, again, is typical of the "function creep" affecting the jobs under discussion. In her view:

> It's not really at the stage where we have to have a separate Twitter shift or anything like that. But if we want to do it properly – if it turns out to be something that's going to stick around and isn't just a fad, then we have to look at incorporating it formally into some kind of work flow system. Right now it's just something that a handful of us do throughout the day . . . It doesn't take long. It's just a matter of remembering to do it.

Belinda's comments reveal a succession of accommodations to new job requirements. Wondering whether Twitter could be a fad, she seems unable to realize the extent to which it has become part of the basic infrastructure of her working day. Like several employees in the study, she excuses a temporary multiplication of labor brought about by technology as something merely passing. The amount of time devoted to Twitter is discounted as a small exception to be assessed for its long-term impact in due course.

The cumulative effect of this "state of exception" becomes clear when noting how many other new technologies Belinda took on board during the study. When we first met, she was one of the few workers who had resisted being on Facebook, but by the time of our second meeting she had joined. TypePad was another platform she had learned in order to maintain the opinion site, and she admitted to using it from home as the need arose. Finally, following her promotion to Acting Executive Producer, Belinda had taught herself the entire production system behind the broadcaster's website, mostly "through trial and error." In each case, she was able to keep pace with job-related technology without formal training – as long as the labor of learning these skills was pushed into her own personal time.

In *State of Exception* (2005), Giorgio Agamben describes the temporary suspension of the usual rule of law under conditions of sovereign threat. When state sovereignty is in danger, nations develop strategies to justify heightened and/or extended powers to withstand extraordinary danger. Adapting this notion, Belinda's story is one of several in this study that can be read as a workplace-oriented "state of exception," in which labor claims have been suspended as a result of technology's unique properties. As we'll see shortly, an inability to see technology use as structurally imposed leads to a lack of clarity among workers as to its limits. The normal working day is suspended in order to maintain the required outputs.[5] Belinda's sense that Twitter might be a passing fad overlooks the reality that in the present work environment, some other communications platform can only take its place. There will never be a time when adapting to new technology will not be a part of her job description in future.

Up to speed

As a recent graduate, Belinda was well positioned for the online workplace. Like Patrick, she had taken her job with the broadcaster as an extension of a work experience placement, and an interest in technology was a beneficial fit for the changing requirements of the organization. This was in contrast to those – particularly older – workers in the study who simply gave up trying to keep up to date with technology as it developed. These workers were often in senior management roles that were less dependent on technological expertise. Clive commented:

> My problem is I don't have any time to use the damn stuff . . . I would love to be able to have the time to explore this technology and where it takes you . . . it's a frontier I'm not exploring, and I ought to be exploring, because there are worlds behind worlds behind worlds.

A generational divide characterized the forms of expertise that were valued in information jobs. A senior group, represented here by Clive, continued to operate on an earlier model of accumulated experience and reputation to enter the management hierarchy. But, in Belinda's case, employees were rewarded for demonstrating flexibility and continually upgrading skills to fit with new operational priorities. In between these two models were the workers coping with the transition from one career reward structure to another.

Tanya, a few years older than Belinda, worked part time for the library as a project officer. As someone concerned with information dissemination and retrieval, she welcomed the introduction of wikis, blogs, and podcasts to the workplace since they gave access to so many new ideas. But she consistently worried that she only had "a limited time" to work out how to use them. Tanya wondered if her age was a natural impediment to doing better at her role.

> I keep thinking to myself that social networking . . . it's just getting good at it enough and knowing enough about it to have it fully

integrated into your whole life. But you need that initial time. It's the catch 22 of learning about it so that you can integrate it, do you know what I mean? Or maybe 'cause it doesn't come naturally to my age group or something, I dunno . . .

I'm thinking already on holidays I want to sort out more podcasting, subscribe to more things, I'm going to sort out more RSS feeds – because I think in the long run if I do that it'll actually save me time. But I just am so busy doing your day-to-day kind of stuff that I haven't actually had time. I subscribe to a lot of online things, but I can see now people are changing from that to more like your feeds and stuff. And I thought that will be good . . . it probably doesn't even take much time, but I just haven't been able to sit down and do that.

Tanya seemed almost paralyzed by the amount of advance publicity accompanying new technologies that she knew were full of untapped benefits. Her desire to learn more about online culture was exacerbated by the knowledge that all of these innovations were designed for convenience. There was irony in her feeling that she didn't have time to learn how to use these time-saving devices. Tanya's responses were indicative of a wider problem to do with the pace of technology adoption expected in the workplace: "I feel like I'm storing all this up, and then I'm thinking 'What, to do on my holidays?' And then you feel resentful and think hang on, something's wrong here." Her colleague Donna had a similar attitude: "all these things take time. If I've got time I should be jogging around the park not sitting at the computer for the rest of the evening. It's boring," she concluded. "One long day at the computer. You can just absorb your whole life in work and not do anything recreational."

Such comments highlight how the democratic benefits of the participation economy rely on particular habits that don't suit all workers equally. Those at the forefront of technology use are typically young, white, and male, with the time to maintain regular multi-media use.[6] For workers like Tanya, additional time is needed to become literate in online technologies before their benefits can be obtained. Meanwhile, Donna is representative of many employees who need to be convinced that investing their time in learning new technologies is beneficial when their schedules are already stretched. As working mothers, these responses also suggest that gender plays a role in accessing the affordances of participatory media. In fact, Tanya had been feeling "behind the eight ball" in regard to work-related technology as far back as her last period of maternity leave – 12 years ago:

there were so many changes in technologies while I was away, I felt like the whole world had left me behind. And I actually made a conscious effort and spent heaps of time and signed up in my own time and did some courses in the new technologies, 'cause I just – I hate that feeling of not knowing what I'm doing. And all the Internet and everything had come in while I was at home.

Here the rate of workplace change poses a particular disadvantage as commitment to childcare prevents the ongoing accrual of technological competence. Now, Tanya was finding the timeframes for keeping up to speed even more challenging: "huge things are just happening all the time," she felt, and this was further discouragement from taking time away from the office.

The difference between Tanya's experiences and those of Belinda from earlier might be understood as the perspective a career break provides. Belinda hadn't left the workforce for any significant period, and had become accustomed to the expectation that she would need to update her skills regularly to stay on top of her job. Later chapters will highlight how this affected her ability to manage workplace demands as she ascended the career hierarchy. It is hardly incidental that an increasing number of responsibilities kept her busy enough to prevent any genuine assessment of the number of technology platforms she had been asked to adopt, and how they affected her workload. By contrast, Tanya's time out from office schedules served to reinforce how quickly things had changed, and how difficult it was to keep step with developments. But of all the workers in this chapter, only Tanya sees her struggle to adapt to the workplace as a reflection on her own ability. Her decision to stay home with children is the principal reason she feels left behind by technology – it is never a matter of organizational strategy.

Other workers reinforced that age and gender were not the sole determinants in coping with technology roll-out. Pam, a 29-year-old librarian, was also feeling the effects of her employer's new publicity measures in the duration of the study. Initially hired to work for the library as a collections officer, Pam's job involved acquiring, filing, and storing material gathered from donors. Though it wasn't a particularly challenging role, she liked the fact that it could be confined to set office hours. Pam's job suited her quiet personality. While she needed to call and meet donors individually at times, her work communication was generally confined to sending email, which she preferred over talking on the phone. A number of initiatives in the library were altering these arrangements, however. The introduction of a weblog for the heritage collections was the first of these changes.

Blogging about the library's acquisitions was thought to be a way to enhance public awareness of the resources and facilities on offer. The library was also turning to new technology to improve feedback avenues available to clients. Pam had been placed on a reference desk for the library's general collection to answer inquiries from visitors, and this role alternated with a phone roster that had been expanded to include instant messaging.

Pam admitted that these new platforms made her feel nervous, since they involved much more spontaneous contact with the public than she was used to. Overall, she was finding it hard to manage the growing list of expectations. "They're not reducing any work-load," she said. "They're just giving us more stuff to do." In her view, "You kind of think something has to give, you know, you can't just keep piling work on us." To begin with, Pam had felt capable doing her job, but the increase in tasks made her feel "more stressed." "I feel worried as well because I want to get it done and I want to do it well."

The library's expanded online services were part of a broader outreach program that included a significant events calendar capital-izing on its new and improved location in the middle of the city. These public programs were designed to provide entertainment and transparency so that the public would be attracted to learn more about the library's facilities. This outward focus was clearly predi-cated on the transformative properties accorded to participatory culture. As a publicly funded institution, the library saw similar opportunities to the broadcaster in using online platforms to extend its services to and contact with the community. But the effect of this change was to take emphasis away from the craft at the heart of employees' professional identity: collecting and archiving, in the case of the library; radio journalism, in the case of the broadcaster.

Here the lack of distinction between public service ideals and the consumer framework underpinning notions of online participation has clear effects. For employees who had deliberately chosen a job that matched their professional skills and preferences, online work meant a significant change in persona. Pam could no longer keep her contribution to the library "behind the scenes." Like Belinda, she was encouraged to perform her role in dialogue with the public. Pam expressed her own critique of participatory tenets, worrying that the library was changing to try to appear more "glamorous" to an imagined audience. She feared that the work involved in main-taining the collections wasn't considered "as important" by manage-ment. Adjusting to these new conditions, she was showing signs of cynicism at the end of the study, acknowledging, "whatever they say up there we have to do."[7]

The essence of youth

If organizations over the course of this period were evidently seizing upon social media as a source of reinvigoration and relevance, this was also a response to the strength of association between Web 2.0 and "youth" (Driscoll and Gregg 2008a, 2008b). A project officer for the library captured this perfectly when describing her current assignment: "because it's a youth-based project we're using Web 2.0 applications . . . we've got a MySpace, we've got photos on Flickr, we've got a Bebo . . . and luckily the consultant runs that for us." Emerging online platforms were viewed as a series of brand names for employees to memorize and master to prove their credentials. This perspective neatly fit the corporate logic infiltrating both public and private sectors as specialist "consultants" were hired to interpret and navigate new media trends. The formula that had emerged to renew brand relevance and improve relations with youth was also evident in the comments of workers seeking to distance themselves from these very perceptions in order to assert professional credibility. In her contract job as an arts worker, Sam expressed a "gut hatred of the term Gen Y and everything that it relates to," especially when this involved a "fetishization of young people and technology." But when she was offered a job developing an online component for an arts festival program in 2008, Sam faced a challenge. She flatly rejected the assumption that Web 2.0 technology would appeal to her peers, and in doing so found it necessary to distance herself from the very clichés contributing to her position being available.

For Sam, the idea of doing an online festival for youth was "just really really gross," a case of the organization using new media to promote itself as being innovative "when it's really just replicating a lot of stuff that's been done before":

> Initially I was kind of like blergh . . . I really don't want to do that. But then I came up with an idea of what I *would* do if that was what I was doing, and that's what I proposed to him and then he accepted that.

On starting the job, Sam's concerns appeared to be founded as a massive government firewall prevented her from using some of the basic online resources necessary to communicate with her contacts. In this context, the irony was that: "I was hired to provide an arm of the festival that engaged with online culture and new media kind of stuff and I don't have access to a lot of it." The public image sought by the festival – of being in touch with social media trends – faced problems in application:

> a lot of the time when I'm trying to research something the websites I need to access won't be accessible. They'll come up as a commercial website, which they are, but it's because I'm going to pay them money to come here and do stuff, you know?

Blurred distinctions between public outreach and commercial transactions frustrated Sam's efforts to take her employer's intentions in good faith. The further difficulty she encountered was actually contacting her connections in the international art world to make the project a success. Firewall restrictions on the workplace server prevented access to Skype. In order to contact overseas artists in an efficient format she inevitably had to use her own home network – an Internet service that her short-term, contract job was little help in providing.

The festival's enthusiastic embrace of online technologies and their assumed youthful demographic stretched to the point of employment but not infrastructure support. Sam was left to feel grateful for her position at a time when the festival itself appeared vulnerable to financial fluctuations, but a lack of access to the websites and services central to her role reinforced her marginal status. There was more than a little hypocrisy in the festival's desire to make use of the affordances of new media platforms. As Sam was forced to conduct major components of the job in her own time with her own resources, publicity for the festival claimed it was demonstrably in touch with the needs of today's youth. In this case generational stereotypes were the basis and constraint of working in "creative industries" seeking to tap the zeitgeist in only the most superficial way.

Universities were also guilty of strategic uses of social media, at the forefront of efforts to capitalize on young people's assumed preference for online contact. Throughout this study, marketing resources were dedicated to building stronger connections with students and alumni, particularly through sites like Facebook. "Flexible" course delivery and online tutorial participation were just some of the measures introduced to meet the demands of "digital native" Generation Y students. The corporate deals assuring brand-name software for teaching purposes intensified the amount of time required of academics who needed to update skills – in their own time – with each new software release. At a basic level, the always-on "Blackboard" (the name of one of the most successful software packages at the time of writing) created a heightened sense of obligation to stay in touch with classes throughout the week. For experienced teachers like Tony, an Associate Professor of Education, Blackboard was a less than pleasing development. Compared with traditional classroom interaction, he saw it as: "one of those constant interruptions to the day ... because people expect an instant response almost – you've got to keep checking." Intermittent contact with students and regular checking for messages extended teaching hours beyond the classroom, indeed the campus, without any changes to workload calculations.

Online branding was also playing out in universities in other ways. In the first few months of my job at the University of Sydney, a robust exchange between colleagues centered around whether or not staff should "friend" students on Facebook. In the resolution to the debate, I was invited to become a "fan" of my own workplace on Facebook, only to be added as an administrator of the page so that I could advertise our fortnightly seminars to the public. Before my department started its Facebook page it already ran an internal announcements email list that all staff and research students received. The department's webpage had a news section where seminars could be advertised, as well as a weblog attached to the site which new staff could have updated had we been given access and instructions. The department's seminars were also advertised through an external, "public" email list which went to nominated "friends" of the department and further distribution lists across the School and Faculty. Hard-copy posters of seminars were printed and sent to guest speakers in neighboring universities each semester, with an invitation for others to attend. Whether anyone who might be interested in attending our seminars could have possibly missed knowing about them through these existing networks is hard to fathom. But the situation illustrates the extent of the problem at the heart of large organizations continually disseminating the same information through changing modes of technology. It is not just that the message is multiplied, which enhances the information fatigue already evident in the dominant uses of email (see chapter 4). Each time the message changes format it also requires new kinds of discursive and technical skill.[8] In any case, my own ambivalence toward Facebook for work purposes is a direct result of hearing the experiences in this chapter as workers were asked to perform a proliferation of additional labors in the context of their respective office jobs. The conceit of the academic who advertises work events on a social networking platform because she imagines her job to be different from others is the operational premise of a new economy seeking untapped profits in the deliberate confusion of friendship and labor. Academics "still find it hard to accept that their workplaces" are the model for the new version of "knowledge capitalism" playing out in an international white-collar market (Ross 2009: 214).

For the large organizations in the study whose remit involved regular communication with the public, what was claimed in many quarters as a revolution in participation appeared as something quite different. Web 2.0 technologies actually equated to a widening suite of additional work demands. On top of an already heavy email load, employees were attending rotating training sessions to learn how to navigate and contribute to staff wikis, digital content delivery services, and online data-processing software. Whether it was contributing to a work blog, answering Instant Messages, or carrying the Twitter feed for the corporation, workers were increasingly coerced into online participation in the name of openness, equity, and transparency. As the platforms became more popular, and their efficiency logics presented as unquestionable, the choice of whether or not one might choose to participate became increasingly slim.

Beyond the already short-lived Web 2.0 hype, these changes raise long-term challenges of motivation and incentive for employees deliberately seeking work in public-sector roles. In the cases discussed here, the external identity of the organization appeared destined to clash with employees' internal work ethic and the values that had secured their original commitment. Universities were one of a range of public institutions that fell sway to PR mantras that social networking could translate to newfound relevance for a generation growing up with digital appetites. But in doing so they lost some of the trust of staff who never imagined they would have to subscribe to the corporate philosophy that friendship communities represent an untapped business opportunity.

Those proficient in online technology set the terms many organizations followed in utilizing social networking platforms as the core territory to capture brand loyalty. Meanwhile, for employees struggling to stay ahead of the global financial fallout, the same social media were sold as the solution to the problems of the contemporary workplace. Dan Schwabel, author of *Me 2.0: Build a Powerful Brand to Achieve Career Success*, was just one of the many advocates claiming personal branding "as career protection in uncertain times" (Levit 2009). Recruitment lift-outs urged employees to develop social media strategies for their companies to prove their value in cut-throat times. But as the recession took hold in many countries, and Australian workers felt grateful to maintain the jobs they had, such optimistic advice could only appear strained. Even uniqueness starts to sound the same when everyone is trying to perform it. "Brand You" was never conceived for a mass audience, not to mention a time when every other mid-ranked knowledge worker was competing for a dwindling number of jobs.

Riding the wave of the social media boom, an overwhelmingly white, male, US-based commentariat failed to differentiate between the commercial imperatives of business entrepreneurs and the very different settings their pronouncements were coming to affect. Punchy rhetoric designed for corporate CEOs and big media companies sounded particularly hollow to the far greater numbers of workers charged with the task of implementing participatory tenets for the benefit of others. By the end of the decade, ambient technologies had left the privileged hands of the digerati and made it into the mainstream, impacting the workloads of mid-rank employees in information jobs everywhere. Workers implementing the new "convergence culture" were expected to tolerate periods of transition as enthusiasm for specific platforms temporarily suspended labor claims. The participatory ethos of new media platforms may have met the service ethics vital to public-sector organizations, but they did so at the expense of the ordinary workers facilitating the exchange between information producers and consumers.

In her article for *New York Magazine*, "Let Them Eat Tweets," Virginia Heffernan was one journalist who took investigative license by following Twitter for a day to get a feel for users' moods. "I wish I didn't have obligations," she noted from one source. "I wish I was rich and had personal assistants." To this, Heffernan added: "Right on. And those assistants, presumably, could do our Twitter work for us." Heffernan's piece was one of the more astute to emerge in a genre of lifestyle reportage endlessly fascinated by the task of domesticating social media. Her story captured the divide emerging between those who could afford to have their Tweets remain whimsical banalities and those for whom the platform was becoming just another part of the job. As web work became a key focus for funding and development in the organizations of knowledge industries, new job opportunities emerged for those – particularly young – workers comfortable with online platforms, and those early adopters with the digital literacy and PR personality to develop consultancy services. But others faced greater difficulty adjusting to these changes as their roles were forced to become outwardly directed to captivate the public.

Friendfarming, Twitterbots, astroturfing, and brand analyzers were the flipside to the forms of friendship and community flourishing in online avenues. In the worst of these trends, web gurus sought to gauge the dollar value of friendship and literally quantify the value of online networks.[9] If employees have little choice but to use communications technology as part of the job – if information work inevitably involves "getting intimate" with clients, employers, and colleagues online – the lesson to be taken from this chapter is that the future is destined to reward those platforms that can continue to mark out space that is distinct from the commercial imperatives of business. Limited visibility options, private profiles, volume settings, and "fake following" provide temporary and individual solutions for workers trying to maintain genuine online friendships when their jobs demand a public identity. What kind of community is being summoned by these outward performances of friendship and secret modulations of intimacy? Perhaps one not so very different from any other. But in an age of online social networking, the point to remember is that an exceptional amount of *work* is now needed to ensure friendship survives the efforts of so many outside interests hoping to "instrumentalize" our connections for the basest of benefits.

Part III

Looking for Love in the Networked Household

7

Home Offices and Remote Parents

Family Dynamics in Online Households

What I do like to do is close the door into here, if I'm not working, because visibly it's kind of a reminder of work, and it feels like a bit of a work intrusion into home. Home ceases to be the sanctuary that it should be, I think, and that is the downside.

Wendy, Television Executive Producer

The previous two sections described a set of structural changes that have contributed to employees' willingness to use new media technology to stay in touch with work. In Part I, these factors included the aestheticization of mobile lifestyles through advertising copy, the hegemony of "flexibility" in management discourse, and an absence of clear workplace policies regarding appropriate response times for email communication. In Part II, the seductions of Web 2.0 platforms were shown to arrive at a key turning point in white-collar employment conditions generally, as job markets became subject to the influence of the 2008 global financial downturn. Online social networking became a means of navigating unstable employment conditions and finding solace from intense and often isolating workplaces. Together, these separate influences exacerbated an already existing tendency among middle-class employees to seek investment and meaning through work (Edwards and Wajcman 2005).

This third section of the book takes the idea of work's intimacy to another level. It makes the more ambitious argument that beyond the influences of management, technology, or the wider economy, employees themselves appeared increasingly willing to engage in work beyond office hours – often to the detriment of other intimate relationships. In addition to the external factors contributing to overwork in information jobs, it is the internal motivations of employees who willingly engage in a lengthening workday that is hardest to explain. This is the admission heard throughout the study from workers like Tanya, the project officer in the previous chapter who was struggling to keep up with the pace of the job. As she explained: "I suppose I could say, look, I just can't get this finished. I mean, there's always that option. I suppose it's probably me, that I want to finish something properly."

The need to get the job done *properly* is one of the justifications we will hear regularly in this section, even though notions of when work is complete appear to be self-imposed. Workers are shown to put the importance of finishing work in advance of other demands on their time, especially as job descriptions expand beyond initial expectations. These chapters move the focus of discussion to the home, to see how work-related technology competes with the pleasures and demands of love and family – and how, in a battle between the two, it is work that often emerges the winner.

Making space for work

One of the major hopes for new media technology was that it would solve the problem of the "absent father" – the parent whose work prevented the experiences and pleasures of watching children grow up. Today professional demands affect both parents, and while technology may allow them to be present in the home, many attest to being engaged in work communication even when they appear to have left the office behind. Miranda was one participant in the study who described her frustration when her husband used his laptop at the dinner table:

> The only time I find there are issues, from a household relationship point of view, is if my husband has the laptop at the dinner table, which he has done in the past and I've gone off my nut . . . I give him the raised eyebrow and put a stop to that one. But he does it from time to time.

Miranda's husband was the Deputy Principal of a local school, which meant "he needed to be on call sometimes." Checking emails at the dinner table was something he did more often "when there's a bit of stress at work." But Miranda's attitude was to ask: "What's

20 minutes? Unless someone's died. And even then they're dead, so 20 minutes isn't going to make a difference." On these occasions, Miranda's daughter would talk to her mother during dinner, given that her dad was proving "non-responsive," and that's when Miranda would "put my foot down and tell him to put it away."

A recurring finding when entering the homes under study was the different gender preferences in where people chose to work. Women would regularly prefer to use technology in areas shared with other members of the family. As Miranda explained: "This is like the centerpiece of the household, this dining-room table." While her daughter did her homework at the table, Miranda would be in the kitchen making dinner: "Then I'll come over here and sit at the laptop and I can work, email, do whatever I need to do. And she's there and she can ask me questions, ask for help." Barbara, the head of the library, also worked at the dining-room table, a preference that had developed early:

> I think lots of people use the dining-room table or the kitchen table to study, and certainly when I went back to study . . . the kitchen

Figure 7.1   Miranda's dining table

Figure 7.2   Kitchen office

table was where the kids were. I feel strangely uncomfortable at the desks upstairs. I mean, it just isn't my workspace.

Men, by contrast, often had a dedicated office away from the rest of the house. Miranda's husband used his study "as a place of escape, especially if he knows there's work to be done in the house." Clive also confined his work to one room that was "slightly isolated from the rest of the house." Clive's teenage children used their laptops in other rooms, and even in bed, to his bewilderment. "Marjorie would divorce me if I did that." Clive used his computer on a desktop only. To be online therefore necessarily separated him from the rest of the family. In contrast to Clive's large, self-contained study, Marjorie had a desk and computer set up in their bedroom. All up there were four computers in the house, and there was little cause for conflict over technology since wireless broadband allowed them simultaneous Internet access.[1]

When he was at home, Clive described his use of technology as "almost a hobby." In these relaxed surroundings, Clive felt more comfortable blurring the lines between work and leisure: "So if I'm doing an email here and then I slip into Facebook and do a quiz on books or something – in a way, I suppose I play with technology more here than I would at work." A recreational element enters the equation as wireless connectivity makes the business of work effortless: "I think we're all sort of habituated to working at different times," Clive mentioned. "I think that's the very bizarre piece of it. When you're home, it's a bit like the equivalent of doing a model railway or being a stamp collector in the past, or something like that." The down side was a sense of physical isolation among family members dispersed across the house, as we'll see with other workers later in the chapter.

Clive's experience was one of the happier examples of working from home. This was partly due to the older age of his children and his relatively senior position in the organization. By contrast, a number of other parents in the study struggled to finish work within the time constraints of office hours, because their children required more interaction at home. In Tanya's case, her part-time status meant that she could finish her formal day at the library mid-afternoon and pick up her children on the way home. These shorter days fit the school schedule, and sometimes Tanya stayed home entirely if her kids were sick or needed transport to appointments. This flexible arrangement was the backdrop guiding her tendency to finish off a report or check her email at home if she felt she was falling behind.

> Because I work till 2:30 to get the kids, I'll often have a 5 o'clock deadline for something so I end up coming home and then finishing something. I don't always do it, but just every now and then it will involve doing a report. And then it's the case of trying to compete with limited space with everybody else.

Tanya recognized that "there's not the explicit expectation that I'm going to do that, it's more up to me I suppose." She acknowledged that she had discussed her extra home work with her partner, who "doesn't think I should be working when I'm not getting paid for it." These tensions often arose when Tanya wanted to work in the home office and her partner needed to be online as well. As a small business owner, Tanya saw it was "really imperative" that her husband was available online: "So yeah, it is a bit difficult sometimes. But just occasionally I just really have to do something and I will throw everybody off, but then that just puts my husband back with his work, basically."

Tanya was beginning to realize that the best way to avoid competition over computers in the home was to buy more of them.

"We've got a laptop as well, and we're just considering getting another one because my daughter's at high school next year and she's using it a lot now." While the laptop was supposed to be her husband's to use, it was the kids that had taken over: "So now he's thinking he'll get another one because he's going to start using it out in the field as well."

Wireless broadband was the technological advancement that helped the family stay online and be together. Tanya was like several working mothers interviewed who used wireless to stay connected online and maintain involvement in other things happening around the house. Tanya described this shift in the dynamics of the house as "a double-edged sword." Wireless allowed her to break free from the confines of the study and move out into shared space, but the quality of interaction seemed to change in the process: "you're with the family but you're not kind of thing."

Partial presence

A number of parents in the study shared Tanya's sense of *partial presence* in the company of family when combined with online connection. As she described it, sharing space with others was "good in that you can see someone and they sort of seem like they're available, but they're not really." In her words: "It feels nice and superficially it looks like everybody's a bit more involved together, but probably the reality is not." An IT manager in the study, Geoff, registered a version of this experience too. Geoff was raising a small family with his wife, Linda, a software engineer. Geoff and Linda met online, and Internet use was a major feature of the household. Linda's work often involved long hours on projects with fixed deadlines: "My wife will have what her team calls a code freeze where they have a certain deadline and they have to meet it regardless of what they're doing. On a Sunday she will be working till 3 a.m. to meet this deadline." Geoff saw this kind of work as one of the negatives of online connection at home, although it was better than having to take a taxi to work, because "she's able to do it here and then just go straight to bed." In the binge culture of coding work, location made little difference to Linda's working hours. Her family had to realize that she was inaccessible during these times, despite her presence in the house.

As for Geoff, his job generated home-based work of its own. His IT position meant that he was obliged to prioritize crisis response during the workday, and commuting to different branches of the

Figure 7.3 Geoff's home office (1)

university added to the time between jobs. Away from his desk for regular periods, most of Geoff's email couldn't be answered at work – there just weren't enough hours in the day. Rather than stay late at the office, most nights he would spend answering email from home.

On the surface, this arrangement is testimony to technology's flexible benefits – giving Geoff the freedom to leave work and still keep up with expectations. In practice, Geoff answered his email upstairs in the home office, away from the family. As such, he noted:

> My kids have kind of learned that they don't come near me really if they know I'm doing something. And the thing is – what really worries me – is that TV and Internet have basically taken over in our house as the primary means of entertainment and interaction.

A specific example captured Geoff's dilemma:

> My three-year-old and my seven-year-old probably spend more time interacting with the computer than with either of us. And that's on a daily basis. My three-year-old, it's scary because she interacts with

Figure 7.4   Geoff's home office (reverse view)

some of those children's websites; the computer will talk to you and sing songs and that, and she'll say hello, and say hello back, so she's actually talking to the computer; it's almost like she thinks it's real . . . So that really worries me because she is there doing that. And I think I'd love to just stop that but I've got to do my own thing. I don't like it, but that's how it is . . . They love playing games I think, but we probably need to rein that in a bit. And how are we going to do that? We're both very tired and we just want to space out our-selves . . . sometimes it's tiring.

A degree of exhaustion pervades Geoff's description of family life. He genuinely worries about the amount of attention he can afford to give his kids, and struggles to generate the energy to engage with them after a long day of work. What's interesting here is that there is a clear relationship between the amount of time the children spend using online technologies and the parents' work schedule. This pattern occurred in other study participants.

Donna worked as a project coordinator for the library in charge of capital assets. Her job involved negotiating between multiple stakeholders, including library management, outside consultants, and building contractors hired to design and build infrastructure. In our first meeting, Donna's schedule was especially busy, as the library was still ironing out issues from its relaunch following a major renovation and upgrade. She told us she had "the highest mobile phone bill" in the organization. During this period she was working at home up to three nights a week, and she would do this "all over the place":

> So if I've got documents I need to refer to I'll perhaps sit at the dining-room table. If I'm just responding to emails and organizing diary entries and appointments and things I often sit on the couch and do it while I'm watching TV or talking to my daughter or whatever. Sometimes I'll sit in bed when I should be sleeping but I can't so I sort of do a bit of work.

Donna was trying to limit the amount of work she did at home, "but if it's going to make my life easier the next day at work it's worth it." This statement captures the essence of why so many in the study claimed to pursue extra home-based work. But it also neatly effaces the other relationships in the household that could be affected by such individual decisions.

We can get a glimpse of the intensity of Donna's workday in the way she describes the difficulty she has adjusting to being home. "I spend maybe an hour trying to get in my head now I'm home. My work's still very on my mind." The days she spent working from home involved less of a transition: "I don't have that whole, Well, I'm home from work, I'm stuffed, I've had the journey . . . It's a little bit softer." Some things helped to ease the adjustment on arrival home from work: "I have a glass of wine and sit on the couch and I just stare at a wall. I put the TV on but I actually don't watch it."

During the course of these interviews Donna reported that her daughter Chloe spent a lot of time on the computer. On one occasion, "She was taking days off school to sit on the Internet and talk to her friends and she wanted to visit them when we were up in North Queensland. She wanted to stay with them! Never met them, considered them to be friends." Donna thought Chloe seemed depressed and withdrawn and had taken her to see a counselor to address the issues. The counselor diagnosed an Internet addiction, estimating that "90 percent of the kids she sees have Internet addiction." In light of the range of comments from the study's participants who diagnosed *themselves* as addicted to email and other online platforms, this seemed significant. Is Internet addiction less of a problem when it affects adults and relates to work? If so, why?

The second time we met Donna, a period when her workload had noticeably slowed, it became apparent that the depression may have had other causes. Having taken some time off for a holiday, and facing a less hectic workload, Donna had started to reflect on the amount she had sacrificed to stay on top of her job. "I think my daughter could have done with me a little bit more at home during sort of Year 11 and 12," she said. "But now it's almost too late, she's finished Year 12, and she's working herself and doing similar hours that I'm doing." Donna continued:

> I think she could have really done with a lot more support at that time . . . because I've only got a small family as well. But my partner who works a lot of night shift and he does a lot of hours every week and usually has 12 to 14 hour days and sometimes seven days a week. So it's not like he'll notice because he's not there either.

When she was busier, Donna admitted: "I was never home for her after school or anything. It's like I had other pressures on my mind when I probably could have had hers on my mind a little bit more. She had sort of personal issues at the time as well that I could have concentrated a little bit more on." It was here that Donna revealed: "Three of her friends committed suicide during the last six months of Year 12. Yeah . . . and all separate . . . and yeah, that sort of . . . I could have been there a little bit more for her." Perhaps focused on work, and the specifics of our interview questions, this was a detail not mentioned in relation to the counselor visit and diagnosis the first time we met. For now, Donna was thankful that Chloe had found a job and a boyfriend and seemed "well adjusted" overall.

Donna shared some of Geoff's anguish in saying "you do what you can do" raising kids. She acknowledged that she loved the work she had been doing at the time of her daughter's troubles, "so it's sort of like you do it to yourself." The comments were all the more poignant in this interview because Donna was expecting another baby. While she still loved her job, she claimed, "my balance is much better these days and I'll never go back there again. I've learned."

Work as the new family?

Regardless of Donna's success in keeping to a new regime, we can gain insight into the broader phenomenon of work's intimacy through her story. One of the factors she acknowledged to be central to her previously long hours was the bond she'd made with her colleague:

> the other person I worked with was very passionate and a workaholic with you know, no partner, no children . . . a single person, a career-minded person and she was fantastic. We just drove through everything.

> I don't work with her any more. We're still very close and we still talk a lot . . . I sort of love and respect her to death.

In spite of her words to the contrary above, Donna also admitted that "if I had to work with her again I'd probably end up doing the same thing." These contradictions are worth mentioning because they highlight how work-based relationships generate their own kind of intimacy, with accompanying benefits for self-esteem and motivation. In Donna's words: "you're enjoying what you're doing and you're running on adrenalin." The job gave her a regular feeling of importance and achievement that was hard to attain at home, especially with her partner regularly absent. Describing her new role, Donna's tone had the character of mourning that accompanies the end of a major relationship: "There was a while, there was a period of a couple of weeks there where I just wondered what I was doing, the phone wasn't ringing there and I wasn't coming in as much." We could also note the hint of emotion in her realization that: "Even though I have someone to report to in this new building project, no one really cares where I am."

For Donna, like a number of study participants, work was a source of fulfillment that rivaled that of family life. It took priority in daily concerns to the point where other relationships could sometimes be neglected. While this may have been expected in some of the more senior positions in organizations, it also affected staff in a range of less commanding roles. Barbara, the head of the library where Donna worked, revealed that the week prior to our interview, her son had been taken to hospital and she hadn't even known:

> I was about to go home and Therese said: "Harry is in hospital." And I said – "What?" She said – "I thought you knew . . ." She'd obviously said he'd rung or something and was going up to the hospital and he had an emergency appendicitis [*sic*]. So occasionally I can be a little flippant about my family and they do come somewhere near the bottom of the chain.

Barbara put her momentary lapse down to the fact that at this stage in her career – her kids were older – she tended to devote less time to them due to their age. For workers at the other end of the cycle, the decision to have kids was considered in careful relation to work obligations.

When Susan became pregnant with twins, she saw it as an opportune moment to invest in a wireless broadband connection. As the head of a small university department, Susan carried a lot of responsibility in the organization and could already anticipate that her absence on maternity leave would pose a problem for colleagues. As it turned out, her workplace did contact her every day of her maternity leave with queries of one kind or another. Susan's willingness to engage in work during formal leave was admirable testimony to her commitment to the job, but it also indicated the insufficient staffing and planning procedures maintained by her employer. Susan realized that there was no one else around to explain details to her replacement while she was away. Yet her own actions contributed to ensuring that these inadequacies would continue in future.

By the time the twins were born, Susan had developed a reliance on her home connection to stay in touch with work: "I'm a bit obsessive about it," she said, estimating that she would check her email roughly every half-hour. "Even if I'm cooking I'll go and check if I've got another email come through. Is that bad? That is bad." Returning from work at the end of the day, she would take her laptop out on the deck with a glass of wine to answer her email, which was "kind of unwinding while still doing something." Susan was an archetypal multi-tasker – as I realized when she replied to my email immediately one night while also sitting on a conference call. She regularly answered email while watching TV and even when she was in bed.

Susan had decided to stay home one day a week to spend time with her boys, and cut down on the amount of time they were in childcare. Her solution was slightly different from that of the other mothers in the study, who chose to work part-time: "Someone said, why don't I cut down my work to four days a week? I said, well I do more than five days a week work anyway, so why should I not be paid for it?" Susan didn't feel guilty about spending the day with her kids, because she knew she would make up the time later. On her home day she used the time the boys were sleeping to do essential work: "They're only little for so long and I don't want to have them in care all the time, and I know I miss out seeing all these little milestones being achieved."

Susan's arrangement was working as a temporary measure, even though it was harder than she'd expected to work at home with the boys present. On our second meeting she was realizing that:

Even in the first half of the year it was easier. They were doing two two-hour sleeps a day, whereas now we've moved to one sleep and it's not always two hours. It's become more problematic, and they are wanting more and more of my attention at the moment.

Susan was finding that one of the few things she could do while the boys were awake was "answer small emails. Sometimes I can mark some assignments and do a bit of searching on the Web. Anything that requires full concentration, I have to wait until they are asleep." An example she mentioned was how she would try to get the boys playing together: "I get down on the floor with them and get the Duplo blocks out and get them going with that. But as soon as I walk away they want to come. I can't do anything. I find that is starting to become more and more apparent. It's like their awareness when I walk away is increasing."

Susan described her current arrangement as "a bit of a holding pattern":

I'm doing my job and I think I'm doing it well but I'm not extending myself to the point where I could see myself moving. If I'm looking for a promotion in the next year or two, I wouldn't be thinking about that until I could really put more than my 100 percent in.

Susan's perception that she would need to put in "more than my 100 percent" reflects a judgment of the kind of work rate expected of full-time employees in her industry. "I think probably that towards the middle of next year I'll have to face the reality that I want to move forward in my career; I really have to be here every day."

Susan's reflections are a worrying commentary on the choices working women face seeking successful careers in information professions. Decisions about having and raising children are inextricably related to concerns about meeting the performance expectations of a job that seems designed to penalize workers who pursue other obligations. At one point Susan put this straightforwardly:

I think that having children is detrimental to your career. But it's a choice you make because you want to make it. I look at my capacity to work now compared to my capacity to work two years ago; it's remarkably different. For me, it was nothing to get up on a Saturday morning and spend two to three hours doing a little bit of work. By the time 10 o'clock comes around I can say, I've started at seven, I've done three hours, now the rest of the day to myself. Whereas now I can't do that because they get up at 6.30 a.m. and need attention.

There's washing to do and all sorts of additional responsibilities that being a parent gives you.

Susan's situation was clearly part of the territory of having very young children, but it was exacerbated by the fact that both partners were career focused and had moved away from family for work. Thinking back to the discussion in chapter 5, of the social mobility that comes with pursuing white-collar work, in Susan's case moving home prevents regular contact with extended family. This lack of additional support to meet day-to-day requirements actually costs her some of the leisured privileges and benefits of the middle-class lifestyle she may have left home to pursue. While Susan's parents had visited when the babies were first born, it was the ongoing practical support of close relations that might have assisted her ongoing career aspirations. Instead she and her husband managed their work and home lives largely on their own.

Closing down communication

For those with older children at home, the consistent description from study participants was that online technology exacerbated a sense of insularism among family members. For Frank, mobile access to work brought clear improvements to his capacity to manage his job outside the office, but for the family in general he found the effects of online connection to be "nowhere near as positive":

> people do tend to sit down in front of their computers and work or play or do their homework or their study and that sort of thing. So it can be quite insular, the environment. I don't know how more insular it is than watching TV or reading a book, it's just a different sort of activity, really.

Tanya also wondered whether using computers was any different "to all the family sitting around in front of TV." Using the laptop actually felt more active than TV watching in her view. The difference was that with television at least you were "doing something *with* somebody."

> I mean, that's a real thing in our family. My daughter came in the other day and said to my husband and my son, do you realize you just – all you do is sit on screens all day. And they do, because his work is full on, and then the hobbies, all the eBay, the YouTube . . . She

actually had to come and say, we're going for a ride. Get on your bike! She really did. She marched in here and told them they're spending way too much time on the screen and blah, blah, blah.

What's lovely about this story, of course, is that the daughter reverses the default assumptions regarding new media use which posit the child as the problem user in the family – part of a wider set of anxieties about young and vulnerable Internet users. Some parents in the study adopted strategies clearly intended to limit children's computer use. Peter, another academic, refused to let his family have broadband for this reason. It was far more common, however, for children to be competing for attention from tired and busy parents, whose own computer use continued on their return home.

Irrespective of their own behavior, parents saw the distracted presence that resulted from computer use as somehow implicated in the erasure of a more valuable form of interaction amongst family members. As Donna explained it:

> We talk less, we all do our own thing on a computer and we all think we're communicating but all we're doing is typing on a computer a little bit. We're not as interactive with each other I think . . . not as active. Whereas we might have kicked a ball around and played with the dog out in the backyard, all that sort of thing.

In Donna's household, the situation was fairly entrenched: "Unless we go: 'Right! No computers!' Which I do sometimes if I get really, really shitty. Take the cord off the computer for a few days. It kills everyone in the house but it's sort of good."

Clive also noted a similar pattern:

> What tends to happen at night time, after dinner and so forth, we all go off to our own rooms and hook up to the Internet rather than sitting down and chatting or whatever we might otherwise have done. If I'm upstairs and Tom is downstairs and we're both online or Marjorie is, I could send them a note, which is very bizarre in a way. It's another way of communicating. So that's changed. We're using the room space more than the living space.

Like the email communication that had taken over from hallway conversations at his workplace, Clive's family was "spending less awake time chatting to each other. We are separate." To engage in conversation meant either sending an email or moving between individual rooms, which inevitably cut down on spontaneous interaction.

There are a number of ways to make sense of the dynamics discussed in this chapter. At one level, the home space appears as a necessary complement to the wider disciplinary regimes of productivity and efficiency emerging from the workplace (Mackenzie 2008). This occurs in addition to wider cultural trends seeking to make personal life and the domestic realm primary locations for the performance of citizenship (Hay 2006; Kipnis 2003; Berlant 1997). The fact that the home office is now an architectural commonplace in so many domestic settings consecrates the idea of a career-centered and responsible citizenry, one that sees fulfillment in the combination of personal and professional success. The home is the place where laboring identities are produced and reproduced on an individual and generational scale. As children grow up in homes with work-focused parents, part of their education is to witness the labor regimes that will be necessary to secure their destiny as middle-class professionals. Middle-class kids become accustomed to white-collar habits from an early age, learning from experience that households are always also workspaces. The mainstream adoption of the home office as a normal expectation indicates that for growing numbers of people, the private sphere now takes on some of the utilitarian considerations of the public. Clive was one study participant who noticed the potential consequences of such a shift. Working from home, "the positives are also the negatives. What is it doing to relationships and what is it doing to interaction and conversation? Is it really meaning that when I come home, the atomized reality of work becomes an atomized reality of home?"

The critical self-reflections that workers ascribe themselves in this chapter offer their own kind of commentary. For Geoff and Donna, an overwhelming wistfulness if not ambivalence seems to attend thoughts of home and its lost chances for intimacy. Both appear powerless to change a situation that emerges from their own willingness to become subject to work's punishing expectations. Susan's thoughts highlight the dilemma facing career-driven women in industries apparently unforgiving of having children. Her experience and evident cynicism prompts us to wonder what kind of world is imagined by workplaces that lead their employees to believe that having a family is a damaging risk. In each case, the mere fact of being at home is no longer a refuge from the cares and concerns of the office. Despite a lot of good intentions, the quality of care parents seem able to grant their outside work relationships is irrevocably affected by attention-seeking technologies. Indeed in many cases, online devices themselves appear to be as demanding and compelling as children. Meanwhile, the next generation of workers grows accustomed to providing entertainment for themselves by way of the same devices. If the long-term effects of these changes are yet to play out, we are certainly in a position to acknowledge the challenge online connectivity currently poses to cherished ideas of domestic fulfillment. As Clive concluded: "it's so immediate and so visually stimulating. Why would you want to exchange it for cornflakes?"

8

Long Hours, High Bandwidth

Negotiating Domesticity and Distance

The previous chapter's investigation of household dynamics is all the more interesting placed in relation to another phenomenon observable during the study. Visiting the workplaces of parents struggling to find time to spend with their children at home, family photos were regular additions to be found on office cubicles and desks. Holiday photos of young children on screensavers were a poignant addition to the very devices preventing more time with kids. These affective tokens were a symbol of the remote nature of intimate relationships, and technology's role in blurring the line between virtual and actual presence. Here the performance of love for family took place in the workplace, where children rarely visited. The photos seemed designed for the benefit of colleagues, or perhaps as a reminder to workers themselves, that whatever captivating power the work world offered, the true object of employees' investment could be found elsewhere.

Building on these changing dynamics of family life, this chapter moves further into the intimate sphere to show how love, romance, and friendship are each reconfigured in the convergence of online technology and the long hours of the professional workplace. Experiences shared in interviews highlight the complexities of maintaining relationships amidst lengthening work schedules. Chapter 2 already showed some of the opportunities to be gained by using communications devices for caring contact. Richard's working arrangement allowed him to spend more time at home with his wife, which ameliorated some of the solitude and separation involved in his international journalism career. Meanwhile, Lisa's morning video call with her baby showed how home life can be accessed in the course of the working day to suit the schedules of parents. This chapter takes these ideas a step further to illustrate how office and home space are each transformed and rendered visible as ambient technologies allow a widening number of companions throughout the working day.

Commentators and marketing departments are among the pro-tagonists to have coined the term "full-time intimate community" (Ito 2007) to describe the select group of friends who bear regular witness to each other's micro-broadcasts online. The extent of this practice is contingent on factors such as age, gender, geography, and culture (Hjorth 2009), in addition to questions of technological infrastructure (Gregg 2010b). In the context of this study, micro-broadcasts can be regarded as a supplementary feature of jobs that require a considerable number of tasks to be conducted by key-board. Status updates are a pleasurable compensation for the lack of physical time available to share with loved ones following the demands of office hours. At the same time, however, other examples in this chapter suggest that the constant flow of email from morning to night can help workers feel valued and involved in a way that may not be obvious in their outside work relationships. In these cases, work-related communication provides a source of investment, intrigue, and ultimately satisfaction that sometimes rivals the plea-sures of domesticity.

The stories that follow offer the strongest evidence of the changes occurring in work cultures as a result of communications technol-ogy. They prompt us to ask, if the romantic notion of love typically involves the desire to spend time with another, can we begin to see the constantly connected behavior of workers in this book as a form of unrecognized intimacy? If employees regularly claim to "love" their work, what does love mean in this formulation, and how seri-ously should we take it as a rationale for the amount of time they choose to spend in its company?

The language of love

Classic definitions of love see the beloved as "the only important thing" in life, compared to which "everything else seems trivial" (Armstrong 2003: 3). John Armstrong's "philosophy of intimacy" notes the combination of longing and rapture that accompanies "the romantic vision," leading to "the sense that one is in touch with the

Figure 8.1 Bringing home to work

Figure 8.2 Domesticity at a distance

source of all value" (ibid.). A significant number of participants in this study spoke about work using language very similar to these tenets. The desire to be alone with work, to the exclusion of all other distractions, was certainly couched in the language of productivity and efficiency in many cases. But, as evidence from the previous chapter shows, the time spent engaged in work-related tasks regularly rivaled or came at the expense of other experiences. There was often little time for the very domestic or leisure pursuits we might consider to be the rationale for needing to be efficient in the first place. Clive and Geoff each lamented changes to family relationships as a result of computer use, even though it was their preferences to work in an office away from the family that contributed to this isolation. Meanwhile, Donna showed signs of being beguiled and enamored by a colleague whose career success was an enticing and infectious adrenaline hit. Susan also valued the times her twin boys were asleep so she could focus on solid work.

For working mothers in the study generally, intimacy with work equates to a kind of reprieve from the demands of other members of the household, a way to reclaim time for different ends. In this sense, work's intimacy translates to mean the solitude necessary to accomplish job-related tasks. It is the contentment to be found in developing habits and dispositions to suit those times of the day with the best prospects to be alone with work. Readers familiar with feminist media studies traditions might discern a synergy here in the desire for solitude these working women display and the kinds of pleasures described in studies like Janice Radway's *Reading the Romance* (1984) and Dorothy Hobson's work on soap opera (1982). These scholars showed how female fans asserted themselves in domestic settings by taking time for leisure and escape in the enjoyment of consuming narratives. By contrast, professional women in this study fight for time to perform paid work pursuits, even if the amount of work performed is poorly recognized by their employers, as previous chapters have indicated. These women are less interested in romance *fiction* since the real romance and adventure is to be found in work. The ultimate romance for the post-feminist professional appears to be the aspiration to "have it all" (McRobbie 2009). For those without a home office – a "room of one's own" (Woolf 1929) – what's notable about this is the gender divide in the study that seemed to grant men more solitude than women in the use of a home office. These spatial practices often said more about the dynamics of domestic intimacy and broader social attitudes to women's career aspirations than the material compiled from interviews, which instead showed how female workers developed tactics to navigate the "cramped space" of home (Morris 1996).

Some workers clearly pursued work with such intensity in the absence of a significant intimate relationship. The demands of the job – or, in the students' case, jobs – served to fill whatever absence this may have represented. But in a number of other cases, work offered a form of engagement and structure that challenged what the domestic realm had to offer, regardless of partnership status. This was evident in workers like Georgia, high up in the library's directorate, who occasionally took the position of Acting Head when Barbara was away. Georgia tried to use technology to obscure the amount she was working and limit perceptions about being online at certain times. Keeping her laptop in offline mode while working at home was one of these strategies: "that way I can do emails and things like that and then they just are sent or synchronized when I get to work and that way people don't know that I've been working on the weekend or what time I've been working." The other participants in the study were hardly fooled by this routine; Georgia was in fact well known in her organization for being an insomniac. In fact it was the expectation of emails from Georgia that generated a lot of the very early morning email checking observable in other workers employed by the library. Here the knock-on effects of one employee's work habits – the pleasure she gained from being at the center of the organization, combined with her newfound love for her BlackBerry – reinforce the difficulties that arise for other workers when intimacy with work may not be a shared prospect or desire.

Jenny, one of the library's part-time project officers, was one worker who monitored email at home in spite of her paid hours to keep up with the habits of workers like Georgia. Recall that it was Jenny's "personal preference" to engage in this extra work and use email to demonstrate her professionalism. But her inclinations also generated self-censure when the behavior got out of hand. Jenny explained that when she spent too long doing work on weekends, for example:

> I'm feeling pretty guilty, usually. I'm thinking, "Oh look, I shouldn't do this; it shouldn't take this long. I said I was going to do 10 minutes. Just contain it." But I then think, No, but it's just easier to get it done on the spot and I can do it in there, and then I don't have to come back to it.

Jenny's guilt at not being able to contain her work indicates that in the moment of encounter she finds it thoroughly consuming: she loses her sense of time and perspective. This is, of course, another symptom of infatuation in a romantic sense. Jenny needed specific strategies to control her relationship to work. She kept her home connection limited to a desktop computer in the study to guard against temptation: "I think if I could search the Internet everywhere, I would."

Jenny admitted: "I do sometimes say, right, this weekend I'm not doing any work," especially because she knew that her partner Mike "would probably prefer I was online less." But she also maintained: "he doesn't truly understand or relate to the idea and notion of the work I do online at home," since "he can't take his work home like I can." A lack of empathy regarding the need to be online at home was the notable fissure in this couple's relationship. Jenny had realized – even though it "will make him sound not very good" – that her partner didn't tend to notice her working habits "when the football season is on":

> Because he'll watch some of the footy, he just doesn't notice that I've disappeared for an hour and a half, but when the football season finishes, he's more like, "What are you doing? What are you doing there?" I'll say, "I'm going just to check my emails for 10 minutes" and I'll come out in an hour, and he'll say, "Why are you doing that? You don't need to do that."

Even though Jenny spent more time working at home than her flexible hours accounted for, she also thought mobile technologies had improved her relationship because she now shared more time with her partner:

> I sit on the lounge. Mike actually made the comment last night, "You seem to still work as much but at least you sit out here now." I thought, I don't know why you think that's any better – because he's watching a movie and I'm doing work – but he seems to think it's nicer.

Jenny's mere presence on the couch – her physical proximity and company – creates an improved sense of intimacy for Mike, even if he is unaware of the labors engaging her attention. The situation referred to here is a time when Jenny was clearing her email inbox on a Sunday night while Mike was watching a movie:

> I finished dinner and everything early and my husband was watching a really bad movie on TV and I was sitting there with the laptop just going through my emails. I deleted 300 emails and it just made me feel very good to start the week like that. I was trying to just do it

all via arrows and enter instead of using the touch pad because I thought the touch pad was louder. He kept keeping increasing the volume of the television and I thought, I'll try and be a bit quieter. I was thinking that I know that I don't have to be doing this work now here. I could watch this movie with him. But I was not interested in the movie and I feel better about a Monday morning if I have done something productive on a Sunday night.

Jenny's efforts to consider her partner by quietly going about her filing are matched by a punishing interior dialogue about why she feels the need to be working. What is it about Jenny's personality that makes her unable to enjoy a trashy movie with her partner on a Sunday night? Something prevents her from being able to view this time and space as free for unproductive activities. The fact that Jenny didn't even work on Mondays is a further complicating factor in this example. Jenny thinks her partner doesn't understand what it's like to have a job that allows her to work outside paid hours. But in this instance it is her own motivation leading her to prefer job-related tasks over his choice of entertainment. Is it that she can't relax, and this is what makes her scorn the film? Is it just a bad film? Or is work actually providing Jenny a beneficial escape from a mundane domestic experience that leaves her uninspired?

Further comments suggested it could be force of habit leading Jenny to multi-task on these occasions given her routine during the week. On Mondays and Tuesdays, when Jenny was looking after her son, it was normal for her to "log onto work and just leave the email open and the laptop on just there and just walk past and check things and deal with things on the fly." A number of Jenny's colleagues, including her boss Georgia, would send her email on days off so that she would be kept aware of developments in the office. It was also so that she had time to think things over before getting to work on Wednesdays. Jenny explained: "If I didn't look at my email before I got in on a Wednesday I think at least the first two hours would just be wasted on catching up." Chapter 2 already discussed this tendency for part-time workers to use unpaid time to stay abreast of work. But Jenny's case was somehow more extreme. A diary entry she sent in following her interview gave some indication of the difference:

Have noticed my partner does get annoyed when I log on at night to check my email. I try to limit it but I sometimes find myself quickly checking my email

- before he gets home
- when he goes to the shop
- when he is downstairs gardening etc.

I check my email constantly because I think to try and stay organized, "on top of things." I do not want any surprises.

The final sentence in this entry reinforces that Jenny's behavior is partly a response to her unpredictable workload, especially the coercive email preferences maintained by her colleagues. But, like other working mothers, her relationship to the technology comes across as a series of opportunities to be seized in moments free from surveillance. Indeed, in this case work reads like a clandestine affair that needs to be hidden from her partner, as if work is a kind of adultery.

Obviously, this isn't the line of thinking people have in mind when they claim to "love" their job. Nonetheless, in a number of examples Jenny's attachment to work directly competes with the other significant relationship in her life. Jenny's story makes us speculate whether working women may be pursuing job-related tasks beyond necessary requirements because it delivers a form of control, a sense of value and accomplishment, which may be unavailable in the context of the home. As was the case with Donna in the previous chapter, being occupied with work can prove an exciting contrast to the ordinary routines of domesticity, or the inadequacies of long-term relationships that may require much more complicated and critical attention.

Ships in the night

Others in the study faced an opposite problem. This was the lack of opportunities to share domestic space with loved ones because of work demands, particularly due to the changing requirements of shift and contract work. The luxury of spending time on the couch with a partner was missing for Arts worker, Sam, who rarely got to see her live-in girlfriend. Sam's partner was a doctor working long hospital shifts that rarely matched Sam's schedule. Filing her radio story alone in the studio at night, Sam longed to be together with Jacqui, especially since the workplace itself was so isolated (see chapter 3). Sometimes she would use her work phone to call home on the few nights that Jacqui was there. She considered the time they had together in the evenings "precious." By the third year of the study, Sam's night classes were creating further obstacles to meeting in this already busy schedule. By this stage Jacqui had started using Facebook to talk to friends on nights at home, and Sam did the same when Jacqui worked late. Facebook friends filled in for the domestic intimacy that absent partners couldn't provide.

Other couples, those with jobs more dependent on computer use, took advantage of online platforms to communicate during the workday. Facebook updates, Twitter tweets, and messenger clients were used to share mood changes, events, and random trivia from distant locations, which partners could witness alongside other friends and family. Patrick and Adam were particularly adept at keeping profiles up to date since their work schedules rarely saw them at home together. In these practices, online space takes on the function of domestic intimacy, in the sense that it is space shared, lived, and practiced with others for a significant period. For those living alone, online friends were the reliable companions that filled the void of a live-in lover or housemate. Online space provided some of the function of domestic relationships if these can be described as the routine pleasures that accompany the more mundane and perfunctory dimensions of the working day.

New media technologies' effects on domesticity occur on at least two levels. First, couples reckon with the possibility of having more knowledge than ever about their partner's daily routine. Time spent at work isn't neatly separate from intimate others, as social media assuage the loneliness and separation of home and market spheres. Meanwhile, returning home from the office, selected networks of friends following online updates have the chance to witness the rhythms, realities, and even shortcomings of others' domestic relationships. Ongoing commentary about home-based activities joins an accumulation of regular posted items as individuals log in more or less often at different times of the week. Online friends therefore have the option of learning the routine of other couples' relationships and commitments. As Sam and Jacqui found, they can even provide a comforting role to keep a friend amused and happy while partners are busy at work. The benefits of online intimacy here include the possibility of expanding the caring capacities and confines of the couple. Virtual friends can assist and alleviate the pressure on domestic partners when work renders individuals unavailable to act as the sole source of intimacy.

This new ambient awareness of both work and domestic routines is not just limited to friends. In some cases during the study, such knowledge worked in the opposite direction, to create workplace cultures more sensitive to personal circumstances. Technologically minded workers would use software applications to determine when colleagues were at their computers, with chat programs allowing for instant visibility, for instance. Others adopted email analytics programs, tools that could chart hours of work according to when emails were sent. Here is Frank explaining his colleagues' daily routines while showing me one such program:

> That's Noel at some ungodly hour working on some project. Graeme . . . he's a late starter. He's not in yet . . . Shelly is an early starter and an early finisher, as her stuff is at the beginning of the day. Someone I was laughing at the other day obviously has lunch. Every now and then you'll find one where someone has this 12 to 1 period where nothing happens.

Frank's job was to coordinate a dispersed team of journalists and web developers from all over the country. By charting patterns of messaging, this software allowed him to observe helpful details about his colleagues' daily habits, knowledge that then allowed him to plan a workflow in response to team-members' typical hours at the computer screen. If this seems an unconventional approach to getting to know co-workers, it highlights technology's potentially useful role in teaching skills in empathy and collegiality in a flexible workplace. In contrast to the masses of email being sent between colleagues in larger offices, where perennially mismatched schedules led to damaging anticipatory affects, Frank's software cut down lag time while also developing sensitivity to the patterns and priorities of others. His was one of few workplaces in the study to use software with sufficient thought to such opportunities and affordances.

Frank's home relationships were also commonly conducted through the use of communications technology. During the day his most regular contact with his wife was by email. Upcoming events and trips would be sent as forwarded messages "you know, because when you are talking you don't sort of pay as much attention to the exact time and dates and places and all that sort of thing." Traveling interstate for work: "Once my bookings are made I sort of forward it to her so that she knows 'Frank won't be here on that night and that is where he is staying' and all of that sort of stuff." Frank acknowledged that communicating with his wife by email "does sound funny," but it was "just as easy" as talking in more conventional ways. Other study participants used MSN to check in with home "particularly in school holidays" when older children lacked direct supervision from the working parent. In each case the technologies worked to improve awareness of different schedules and keep in touch in spite of geographical distance.

Leaving home

Evidence from the study suggests that technology's greatest benefits to domestic life are enjoyed by those with established relationships, households, and jobs. Some of the younger workers interviewed who were yet to develop these commitments provide an important point of contrast. Thinking back to the non-existent lunch break Frank's software detected is to be reminded of the number of workers for whom lunchtime was not marked by any attempt to leave the office environment, whether due to time pressures, a lack of social areas at the workplace, or the absence of colleagues. In the typical seven- or eight-hour day, Belinda claimed, "We don't get up from our desk at all":

> There's a culture in here of eating at our desks; so you go and warm something up in the microwave, and then come back and eat at your desk, which I don't like.

Work and break time – if they were distinguished at all – were separated by the kind of content consumed onscreen. Angela also mentioned eating lunch at her desk, where she would do her "recreational interneting" (chapter 3). Working through lunch, or dining "al-desko," was common enough in office space, although it was perhaps more troubling among those working from home, where the combination of professional and personal life, work and leisure seemed to create a disincentive to leave the house at all. Tegan, for instance, lived in a shared house, and conducted her multiple job roles and Honors study all from home. The "convenience of just being able to have the Internet right here in my room" meant that she could be more "readily available to communicate easily with people." Cutting down commuting time to and from her jobs also gave her an extra two hours to devote to work. The downside to this was: "You become consumed by spending 12 hours a day on the Internet and you study and work when you probably should be like talking to your family or something." For Tegan: "my normal day is get up and turn the computer on before I eat and late at night, because it's like right here." She often thought, after having "all that time on the computer," that "maybe you should go outside and exercise or something." In reality, Tegan spent "the best part of the day, most part of the day, online. Like either studying or like emailing or Facebook." Even though she was conscious that her time might be better spent "going outside," she rarely did so if she was "busy."

Tegan's case was especially noticeable since she was one of the youngest workers in the study. With these habits developing so early in her working life, it set a worrying precedent for the future. Not only did her successive contract positions risk habituating her to the requirements of binge-work, the prolonged apprenticeships relied on substantial unclaimed overheads from running her home office, combined with the general expense of inner-city living. Another concern was that she might develop physical symptoms from such heavy computer use, since this was common in older workers who only came to computers later in their careers. A substantial number of young workers in the study described ailments of one kind or another arising from long hours in front of screens, along with anecdotes about compulsory exercise programs introduced in workplaces only to be abandoned after short-lived enthusiasm.

In the space of just a few years, librarian Pamela also noted changes in her relationships as a result of emerging technology habits. Never much of a phone user, the 29-year-old had the sense that chatting on the Internet was impacting on other kinds of activities. "I don't go out and see people as much because we're already talking on the Internet or SMSing. SMSing is a big thing." With all of this communication happening at home, Pamela observed: "you don't actually meet people, like go out and have coffee with people as much, you know what I mean?" Being in touch with others wasn't an issue. However, the number of new platforms and conduits for intimacy had the cumulative effect of keeping people physically distant: "I stay at home more," as Pamela explained.

Together alone with everyone[1]

These findings take us back to the territory first mapped in this book, namely, the flexibility rhetoric accompanying the emergence of new media technologies. Even though mobile technologies have been consistently marketed to the public as offering freedom from the desktop and the computer, so many users appear to be drawn to screens for increasingly lengthy and static periods. While the particular hardware and software has changed over time, the one constant has been the requirement that employees make considerable use of online technology. For young workers very active on new media platforms, whether by choice or management instruction, the amount of time spent online together on Twitter or Facebook helped to assuage the lack of time spent in physical company in the household. The potential difficulty this posed was when the support structures developed to cope with work-related loneliness came to rival the intimacy originally missed, as in the following example of Patrick and partner Adam.

Coming home from work at the radio station, a job that began before dawn, Patrick would often find the house empty. Taking a nap in the afternoon helped to ease the transition from the pace of work at the broadcaster. Freelance writer Adam also worked in a bookshop, so his hours varied in relation to Patrick's. Nights spent together were contingent on Adam's fluctuating deadlines and Patrick's music commitments. The couple's modest income had them living in a small flat, which also had to function as Adam's workspace. While he originally used to write at a desk in the bedroom, Patrick explained that they'd needed to make a workspace for Adam in the main living area: "it was too difficult for him to try and work and have a space when I went to bed earlier than him." This was one of the clearest examples of work's intimate impact on the home,

Figure 8.3   Bedroom offices

Figure 8.4 Patrick's bedroom office

as different work schedules had knock-on effects beyond the hours of employment. The precarity of contract living involved an additional layer of micro-coordination within the limited matrices of domestic space.

As in Sam and Jacqui's case, technology kept Patrick company when Adam was at work, either outside the home or within it. With his music events to promote and news stories to follow, Patrick had reasons to stay active online beyond his job requirements. Nonetheless, he admitted:

> I do get a pang of sadness when both Adam and I are home and he's on his laptop and I'm on my computer. I just have no idea why that would be the case that we would be both using the computer and be both in the home because, I don't know, we don't get to see each other very much and I don't understand why we'd both need to be working at the same time. Or if it was for leisure, I don't know, I'd rather be doing something else maybe.

Patrick's sense of confusion is exacerbated here as he tries to distinguish between work and leisure as the reason for him being online.

These questions were intrinsic to the professional identity he held as a journalist, in chapter 3, and his use of social networking sites for various forms of paid and unpaid pursuits in chapter 5. Here Patrick also worries that he is failing to perform domesticity the right way. The few moments when he and Adam are able to share proximity and presence brings a new kind of pressure, that is, the pressure to enjoy the ordinariness of home life in its banal and fleeting novelty.

As work separates intimate partners during the day, a feedback loop develops in couples like Patrick and Adam. The consolation of online connection as work takes them away from home leads to habits and pleasures that continue into the night when they are finally together. Domesticity has perhaps lost some of its earlier function, as online friends and contacts become the more regular companions throughout the day. Instead of seeing this negatively, however, and returning to the ideas raised in chapter 5, it is the shared interest in online culture and the kinds of friendships it gives rise to that confirms why Adam and Patrick are so well suited. Placed alongside Jenny's story, which is where this chapter began, this couple understands what it is like to work in the same industry – each being employed in the fickle fortunes of contracted cultural work. One of the secrets to Adam and Patrick's success as a domestic unit in fact seems to reside in this shared belief in the importance of their work, even if it was this "significant relationship" that proved to be the main influence keeping them apart.

9

On Call

Some things are threatened, like the sleep that you need.

Geoff, IT facilities manager

Previous chapters in this book have focused on the day-to-day experiences of salaried, part-time, and contract workers in information and communication jobs to assess the impact of online technology on personal and professional relationships. These stories question the speed with which organizations have taken cues from elite early adopters to initiate changes to workplaces on a broader scale. Conditions of employment in the mid-range office jobs of today's knowledge professions have been significantly affected by the flexibility rhetoric of management discourse that has only been bolstered by the mobile freedoms and participatory tenets voiced by Web 2.0 prophets. Neither of these powerful interest groups has had cause to put the lives of ordinary workers at the heart of their considerations, to recognize the consequences of such enthusiastic pronouncements as they play out in mainstream contexts.

To finish the book, however, it is important to hear from those whose job it is to provide the infrastructure for the practices that have been taken as typical of office workers in this discussion so far. On-call staff are the crucial backbone for the mobile workplace, whether it is the IT support officer whose day consists only of urgent demands – as equipment fails or users lose data – or the PR strategist who fixes the damage as a phone company faces coverage failure. For both, immediacy is key. The job depends on a constant ability to be present when colleagues face difficulties with technology. If other workers in this book show symptoms of anxiety faced with communication overload, and this was often self-perpetuating, these employees' pressures are much more externally driven. For some of the most vulnerable workers we will see in this chapter, the expectation of availability placed on them by management prevents the most commonplace activities, from grocery shopping to gym membership – even the solitude of the daily commute.

These workers' jobs invade the "time of life" to the extent that ordinary activities are rendered precarious. As chapter 3 explained, in recent labor politics, "precarity" has been used to describe the feeling of threat inherent to jobs with flexible conditions that bring an inevitable degree of financial and existential insecurity. For precarity theorists, labor conditions are a battle over a worker's relationship to time. Precarious work involves living with constant uncertainty. In this sense, it captures the experience of "the part-time on-call retail clerk whose non-work time is haunted by the prospect of being called to do a shift, to the self-employed copywriter perpetually juggling contracts, rarely declining a contract for fear of a future lull in the flow of income" (Brophy and de Peuter 2007: 182). The common element is the inability to predict or control working hours, which creates "a contortionist approach to the planning of one's time" (ibid.). Precarious jobs actively prevent the quality of time necessary to maintain personal and social relationships. These "immaterial" factors to do with psychological and ontological well-being are thought to rival the basic "material" issue of financial compensation for hours worked. In the language I have been using in this book, precarity is another manifestation of work's intimacy: its irrepressible invasiveness over one's thoughts, regardless of time or location, is symptomatic of the unpredictable nature of jobs increasingly facilitated by communications technology. Anticipation and preparation for work's *potential* presence are the "immaterial" of "affective" dimensions to work in knowledge professions.

This chapter focuses on workers whose ability to manage time or plan ahead is restricted by the unpredictability of roster systems. Their on-call status restricts their movement in a physical sense as social life and family recreation must be kept within wireless range in case of work emergencies. Returning to one of the book's key themes, it is the notion of "teamwork" that sweetens the demands placed on these workers to meet ever-changing obligations. Yet the stories that conclude this section of the book ultimately show the limits of teamwork's temporary and superficial solidarity.

The one-hour radius

In chapter 7, we met Geoff, the IT manager with two young girls. Travel between university campuses was one of the issues affecting Geoff's ability to stay on top of email, and we noted his tendency to spend time away from his family in the home office at night in an effort to manage this problem. Geoff had taken a new position closer to home by the second time we met. He explained his desire to try "something different" and work on the core computer facilities for another university. The job was at the nexus between IT and facilities management, an area called "infrastructure continuity architecture services." Geoff explained the business of the job was to "focus on resilience and keeping systems going, making sure there's adequate power and cooling." Moving jobs had involved adjusting to a new email system, which was one time-consuming aspect of the move. But the main change to Geoff's lifestyle was an on-call roster. He was one of a team of three on a 7 × 24 roster. Every three weeks Geoff had to be available for work at any time of day. When an incident occurred, a computer contacted Geoff automatically:

> Because we don't have an operations center here, we basically get notified through our equipment, so we have equipment in data centers that will send you a message if something's going wrong, like an air conditioner is failing or if the temperature has gone up too high for some reason, you'll get a message. And it could be any time of day.

The trouble with this system was that there was no way of knowing how important the message was: "that's essentially your job, and you wake up. Getting paid 'on call' basically involves waking up and working out whether it's important or not."

Geoff was feeling "pretty lucky" that he averaged only one call a week each time he was rostered, although "it all depends on the season. When it's a change of season it can really impact on the alarms." Whether or not he was notified, Geoff's schedule had to be organized around the assumption that he might be.

> one of the requirements is that you've got to be within an hour of a computer . . . that's why we have laptops, because we can remote in, and we also have wireless broadband, so we could be at a friend's house or something. For example the week before last I was at my daughters' fete, school fete, I had my laptop with me and I was on the grass logging in.

The organization paid an on-call allowance of $80 a fortnight, plus overtime for when he actually had to do something: "Logging in on your computer is two hours' overtime. If you're just having to phone someone, that's one hour, and if you're having to visit onsite, that's three hours." According to Geoff, there was some tension among staff across the different teams about what was acceptable contact. His own team had agreed to 24-hour contact, but others had not. Though they were paid the same amount per fortnight, these teams only took calls up to 10 p.m. on weeknights and 5 p.m. on weekends. Geoff had agreed to the more extensive contact hours when he started the new job. While he didn't seem to mind the odd call, he definitely felt tired at work the next day when it happened. There was also a safety issue in that the job formally required workers to take a 10-hour break between shifts, or else be paid double. This hadn't happened in the weeks Geoff had been rostered.

Speaking of the impact of the job on his family life, Geoff mentioned that his wife wasn't really disturbed by the notifications. This was because she was typically in another bedroom anyway – their three-year-old daughter had trouble sleeping on her own. So Geoff was often alone if his phone rang at night, and it didn't bother others in the house. The main effect on the family came at weekends, in making plans to do things together. This was because "even though the requirement is to be an hour away, in reality you wouldn't have time to respond." If there were major power outages, for example, "some sort of disaster," Geoff realized he would need to be available "within 10 minutes to actually be able to do something, make a proper decision about what to do. And I guess it's just the way things are." Here Geoff's awareness of the range of potential risks – the lack of air-conditioning in the complex, the warranty details of the equipment, and how expensive they would be to replace – contributes to his sense of responsibility for the organization. It also leads him to be more cautious about contact timeframes than simply accepting the ones suggested by his employer. Geoff limited his movements during on-call periods so that his own actions would never be considered as contributing any further damage in an emergency situation:

> An hour is a bit unrealistic I think. I try to at least have my equipment with me and stay within the capital city sort of thing. We don't go out that much on weekends so it kind of works reasonably well for us, but it is a constraining factor if that's something that I did want to do.

Under pressure

Geoff's experience of taking responsibility for the organization at the expense of his own leisure time was also observable in Belinda, the online news producer described in chapter 6. In her new position as Acting Executive Producer, Belinda was often the only one who knew how to answer technical questions. As the broadcaster expanded its online presence, and a lot of new recruitments were brought on board, she would regularly get phone calls from staff who hadn't been trained sufficiently:

> I get a fair few phone calls asking me how do I do this or how do I do that? Some people have just started. A lot of people would ring me as well as email me. It seems that people email and then if they don't get a response they'll phone me as well. Just to check that I got the email.

She continued:

> To be honest, when I first took on that more senior role in some ways I was pretty proud to be the one taking those phone calls and making those decisions, and that kind of thing. Then I kind of just got used to it and just accepted it. And now when I do get the calls or when I'm expecting to do this or that in my time off, I resent it.

Any glamor to be found in the on-call lifestyle soon wore off. Indeed, Belinda found it difficult to keep work at bay when she needed a complete break. Taking a planned trip to the mountains one weekend, an hour and a half's drive away, she was again contacted by work: "there was still a situation where I might have had to go back and do a shift. I managed to avoid that. I wasn't happy about getting the phone call."

Belinda was aware that the previous EP had left the position suffering burnout. This made her quite conscious of the amount of contact required in the job. The management team was experimenting with different roster systems to try to spread the load. Despite this, her workday felt quite relentless:

> It pretty much starts – like I got quite frustrated this morning because it starts as soon as you walk in. Sometimes I haven't even logged on and I'm getting phone calls and people asking me stuff, and I'm like I haven't even checked my email, I've just sat down, or logged on or anything . . . It would be nice to have half an hour to myself in the

morning, come in and check my emails and have a coffee or whatever and get ready, but that's not reality.

Belinda saw her only alternative option was "to come in really early, and I don't want to do that. So I just have to get used to the fact that when I get in there, I've got to be ready to go." Working in news made it hard for Belinda to plan her time in ways that would be less stressful:

> you can be in the middle of something and then something big will break and you have to drop what you're doing and take on something else. The idea of having a plan to a workday . . . you're just responding to what happens. There's no real way of knowing when it's going to be busy and when it's not. I suppose you learn to cope with a changing work environment. You never really know.

Belinda used technology to alleviate the feeling of anxiety about not knowing what might be happening:

> I never turn the phone off. I don't get that many calls, I just always have to be available to take them. I've got a 3G phone now – it's not an iPhone but I can still check stuff on it. I think I'm expected to be on top of things more and more, to know what my workplace is doing from my phone and check Twitter and stuff. I think it makes me feel more comfortable in the long run, because if I am checking it a fair bit then I know what's been going on. And it's not so much what's going on when I walk into the office, it's what happened over the weekend. If I know what's been happening over the weekend then I'm ready for whatever's coming on Monday. So it's useful from that point of view. The same thing with Twitter. I've used it at home to keep on top of various things, breaking news or whatever, stuff that's happened with the site that I might need to know.

In Belinda's job, as we saw with Patrick, knowing "what's going on" was "part of the skill set." Keeping on top of news stories on a given day was the major challenge, and success depended on learning to manage that pressure:

> I've recognized that you can't know every single story that's going on. Across the network, we probably send out about 300 stories a day. So I can't possibly know everything that's going on with my site. I used to find that quite frustrating but now I don't really care.

Belinda's realization that she "can't possibly know everything" is important in the wider frame of this study. She is one of few employees to directly comment on the sheer amount of information produced by her company, and the impossibility of staying abreast of it all from her one role. It is simply beyond human capacity to be able to know everything that is happening in the organization. Once this point of clarity is reached, and Belinda concedes her limitations, she is able to prioritize her time and focus on tasks that matter. She is also able to appreciate how the workplace contributes to feelings of anxiety:

> There's a real atmosphere of oh, if you don't know what's going on then you mustn't be doing your job right . . . if everyone else is constantly switched on and working extra hours for no extra money, you're like well maybe that's what I should do.[1]

The longer Belinda spent with the organization, however, the more entitled she felt to leave work on time: "I'm not under the illusion that the corporation's going to appreciate it or anything like that. I get paid to be there and I know that I'm still available to be called at any time, so why do I need to be there extra?"

Not working out

The demands of journalism are certainly high given the tremendous appetite of the 24-hour news cycle – another way that communications technologies have affected professional practice. But if Belinda displays a fairly successful transition to management in her ability to transcend some of this pressure, the wider point is that this same combination of perceived availability and urgency applies across job sectors and roles. Jodi was a marketing employee with the telco company in the study. At 26, she was among the youngest workers interviewed. Jodi developed specialized marketing campaigns for particular consumer "segments," as part of Holly's team. Her task was to design ads for telco products targeting women, and the team had been experimenting with social media sites to create "profiles" describing their principal users.

The first time we interviewed Jodi she was enjoying working from home once every few weeks. These were times she was allowed to focus on her "development goals," coming up with ideas on "how we can improve the business." These were days when Jodi was encouraged to think about the big picture, to be "less operational and more strategic." Over time, however, she'd noticed that recurring meetings were starting to affect her chance of having the occasional day at home. In one instance, a last-minute focus group was organized for the day she planned to stay home; on another, Holly "set up a meeting where she wants us all to brainstorm on a design room where we all write on whiteboard." These last-minute developments amounted to a coercive presenteeism that was proving frustrating for Jodi given the conditions she had assumed were in place. The examples she described offered a sense of the pace of work in her office, and the speed with which events were scheduled. A typical day had wall-to-wall meetings: "you have half an hour break and then you run to another one, or you have one that goes all day."

On days she did manage to work from home, Jodi claimed she would have her email open an hour extra at each end of the day, from 7.30 in the morning until 10.30 at night: "Just because I'm addicted to it and I have to see and respond to everything because often a lot of urgent things come up." Even though she cherished working from home to get away from the office schedule, like Jenny, Claire, and Susan, Jodi felt obliged to stay connected nonetheless. Putting an "out of office" message on her email sent the wrong message, she felt:

> if you put an "Out of office" on saying "I'm working from home today and not available on email," then they'd be like "Well, how are you working?" People don't understand that you could just be working on a project when you need to just spread out and think.

Another reason Jodi monitored email around the clock was because on any given day it was the principal source of directives from superiors asking for tight turnarounds.

> Like this morning . . . I planned all this stuff I needed to get done today and then something came up this morning that needed to be done by close of business at eight, and it was going to take up quite a bit of time, so lucky I saw that email and responded to it and was able to manage it and get it done before close of business today.

Rather than an "addiction," Jodi's use of email is here a matter of having learned to prepare for perceived emergencies, and adapting to the communication preferences of more powerful colleagues in the organization. With her managers so often in meetings, face-to-face contact was rare, and email was the one constant in a chaotic schedule.

Like Geoff, since our first interview Jodi's role had changed to include being placed on an on-call roster in addition to her regular duties. For 48 hours every fortnight, she had to be available for conference calls to deal with critical incidents affecting the company. Service faults and coverage issues were among the key problems. Our meeting transpired in the middle of this period:

> I was on-call all day Sunday, Monday, and today . . . I was on a tele-conference last night until 7.30, and I was on one again at 8 a.m. on the train this morning, and I was going to go to the gym in my lunch hour and I got called to another business bridge, and these are just urgent things. We have 20 minutes' notice that you have to hop on, and they're critical incidents that are happening to our customers and we have to work out how to manage them.

Jodi was conscious of how this new requirement of her role was affecting her usual routine:

> it's really hard for me to have that work/life balance when I – like I was doing my conference call last night while doing the groceries and driving to the grocery store, and this morning trying to do it on the train with all these people, customers around me who are not sup-posed to know this confidential customer incident. And then, you know, again trying to have some balance in your lunch hour with some gym, and that doesn't ever happen. I've had a membership for six months now and I've gone maybe for the first two months, and then I had it scheduled today to go and then a bridge was called in the middle of it. So I couldn't go.

The sense of urgency and unpredictability involved in her new job obligations made it difficult for Jodi to make the simplest of plans. Her efforts to place limits on work's invasiveness read as a series of traps or enclosures, as work follows her at every turn once she leaves the office.

The precarity of not knowing when work would be required also affected her home life:

> I had to keep my mobile on last night because they told me at the 8.30 bridge they were going to call one at 6 o'clock in the morning. So normally I would have my phone on silent and only turn it on when I woke up, but because I knew this one was coming, I had to have my phone on so that – I didn't sleep very well, actually, and I had this by my bedside and I was just thinking about this stuff I had at work and I had to get up, about 3 o'clock in the morning, and write down the things that were running through my head that I had to do for work because my head was racing with all the stuff I have to do and I couldn't relax until I'd written it down and my mind could forget about it.

Like her colleague, Claire, Jodi was finding it hard to wind down and rest easily at the day's end without a lot of work-related issues running around her head. Awareness of the technology by her bed made it difficult to fully relax. While Claire learned to close the lid on the laptop – and put it to one side on weekends – Jodi found it harder to distance herself from work's intimacy in the home.

To make matters worse, this on-call extension to Jodi's job was unpaid. It was a mandatory add-on for an indefinite time, justified by the fact that the telco was going through "a five-year transformation period":

> We're migrating our customers from one platform to another and things happen all the time, like ten a day, incidences of things going wrong. So one example this morning was 100 per cent of our systems were freezing and they couldn't do any transactions at all, at all. So whenever a customer comes in: "Sorry, can't help you; system frozen." We had to develop a work-around and some comms for our staff to be able to tell customers what to say in the situation.

Jodi acknowledged that these improvements to the company were unavoidable:

> The annoying thing is like it's not something that you'd ever get recognition for or not something you're going to make the business money; it's just something that has to be done and we just have to do it as part of our job.

Even though she hated the extension to her role, Jodi modulated her frustration by saying: "my manager's also on-call, so she understands what it's like, so that's something." Of course, this neglects to appreciate that Holly was paid a higher salary for this level of responsibility. By contrast, Jodi had simply been told: "Someone has to do it and you're the one that's skilled to do it." Jodi's relatively junior position gave her few choices. While she would be entitled to time off in lieu, she seemed unlikely to claim back the hours. Too much individual complaint would look like trouble-making in this team-based workplace: "I haven't heard of anyone asking for it. I think if I did ask my manager would probably say 'Well I'm doing it and I haven't asked for it,' so I don't think so."

Here is one of the clearest illustrations from the study of a worker who seemed unable to contemplate power relations in the workplace. Jodi appears placated by the logic of the team, unable to match her legitimate grievances to others in the workplace. Jodi's story confirms Andrew Ross's prescient observation that "unlike in a traditional corporate organization, where it primarily affected only the senior managers and executives, today the 'biohazard' of always-on responsibility for the organization affects even the youngest and freshest employees" (Ross 2003: 19). As it happened, Jodi wouldn't have the chance to claim her time off. Within a few months, it became clear that the five-year "transformation period" for the company also involved offloading 800 workers across the country. Given the size of the employer, and the context of the financial crisis, news of the redundancies leaked to the media before staff were notified.

Jodi was on holiday at the time the changes were being announced. Despite this, manager Holly called to give her the news directly, to prevent the possibility that Jodi would hear rumors before returning to work. As Jodi explained: "I was on a holiday trying to relax and then I heard that and I knew I wasn't going to hear anything till Monday, so that actually didn't make me relax. I was wondering whether I was going to have a job or not." By the time she got back to work, "people were still finding out over the phone whether they had a job or not." Jodi was one of the few in her team to survive. Holly was one of the casualties.

Given what we know of Jodi's job conditions, it's perhaps understandable that she actually wanted a redundancy – something she admitted afterwards. With her job restructured and a new manager in place, Jodi started searching for other work. The disintegration of the team had significant bearing on her decision: "I'm not going to stay because all my friends had left anyway, you know?" Soon she was offered a job on a much higher salary working as a marketing manager for a successful childcare company. Leaving the telco, Jodi had little inkling that this business would create headlines of its own shortly after. News of the company's dubious financial foundations was exposed, causing stock prices to plummet. The firm swiftly went from stock-market darling to fully fledged receivership.

Jodi had survived one round of redundancies only to lose her job in another. In early 2009, she was looking for work in the height of the global economic downturn. The main problem she was facing was keeping abreast of closing dates in the struggle to beat other applicants. Advertised positions were closing "within four days of listing" because so many people were looking for work. Jodi was finding that "there's not a lot that I'm actually perfect for":

I'm either over-qualified or under-qualified. There's not much in the middle range because I think that's the people they're getting rid of in these economic times. I'm kind of at the senior marketer, junior manager level which is the level that people are really trying not to employ, just going with the juniors who do the work and the senior managers who control the company, and making do without middle management.

As we've seen, Jodi's junior role at the telco was one of the main reasons for her exploitation. She also accepted additional work as part of her felt responsibility to the team, along with several of her colleagues. It was only now, faced with unemployment, that she had an opportunity to reflect on the past few years of work. Jodi was forced to acknowledge her position in relation to a much bigger pool of employees with similar ideas of their "management material." Outside the cushioning support of the team, hers was just another CV to be processed:

> I'm starting to realize I might have to go down almost 50 per cent of what I was getting paid, maybe even less, because there's just so much competition out there. So many other marketers have been made redundant from companies because it's a support service and it's the first thing to go when the economy's having a bit of a rough time. All the people I know are looking for jobs, like all my market-ing friends are all still looking or they've just found something, or it's taken a long time.

Facing these prospects, Jodi even seemed nostalgic about her time at the telco: "I did have it good." In the space of a year, the same job changed from being unreasonably demanding to better than the alternative.

Workers in this chapter were just some of the hundreds of thou-sands who were subject to a performative display of belt-tightening by large organizations as economic forecasters heralded the biggest downturn in financial history. Jodi's comments fit a wider cultural context in which employees were increasingly being told to accept that any job was better than no job. In 2009, reduced hours, extended leave, and job-share arrangements were the quick fix to a market wipe-out that threatened to take ever more workers as casualties. When this study began, a strong public discourse about "the skills shortage" had seen firms struggling to provide the flex-ible work arrangements and boutique preferences demanded by skilled, educated employees. Within 18 months, the context had changed so quickly that managers were being congratulated for forcing staff to stay away from work on unpaid absences in order to keep their jobs.

Such measures were a bulimic corrective to the intensity of work-loads that had accumulated over a longer period. Crisis conditions only served to consecrate the permanent "state of exception" for labor claims in office cultures that had never come to terms with new media technologies' cumulative effect on workloads. The fallout in Jodi's workplace – over half her colleagues were retrenched – underscores how agreeing to unrealistic workloads out of loyalty to the team is no protection against cost-cutting measures that are decided much higher up. Indispensability is an illusion in an era of strict efficiency targets and mass outsourcing of jobs, where company flexibility comes at the expense of the individual. The bind of today's white-collar professional is to be invested in work as and when required but without the reciprocal assurance from employers that commitment will be rewarded. Such a scenario risks losing the goodwill of employees permanently, as Miranda, another survivor at the telco, explained:

> Nothing is certain in this environment. I think anyone in the corporate environment at the moment would be mad to think that their job was secure, moving forward . . . Never ever assume that you've got a job for life or a job for 12 months.

Miranda anticipated that. with the new changes, "we've probably got about five months' grace, nothing major's going to happen until they get a new CEO in." After that "there'll be a lot of seek.com. au going on again."[2]

If Miranda describes the precarity of employment in present economic conditions, Jodi and Geoff represent the extreme end of always-on work cultures. They show the significant personal costs involved in servicing and maintaining the platforms that deliver the new flexible workplace. Their stories are an important supplement to those of other workers in this book who choose to work more often than formally required and rely on a substantial technical infrastructure to do so. What remains to be determined from these combined perspectives is whether any kind of solidarity can be gleaned from understanding the shared conditions of labor in information jobs. This will be the basis of the conclusion.

Conclusion: Labor Politics in an Online Workplace

The Lovers vs. the Loveless

I think I haven't yet transcended emails. I would like to transcend emails. There is a life beyond email which I think we need to rediscover.

Clive, University Professor

In a global labor economy that continues to be inflected by inequities of gender, geography, and race, the conditions of workers in information, communication, and education industries are hardly the most exploitative. Compared to the genuinely outrageous and toxic environments in which the desperately poor spend days and nights in and out of gainful employment, the overwhelmingly white, middle-class, wealthy, and healthy workers in this study summon little sympathy. A major motivation for this project has been to better understand a situation in which so many educated professionals remain protected from an awareness of others' brutal working conditions in the course of busy day-to-day priorities. This is to ask how even the most ordinary job commitments can appear to blow out of proportion at the mere sight of an overflowing inbox.

At the outset, it seemed plausible to wager that the "social ethic" (Whyte 1963) of white-collar workers may have been the rationale for spending long hours at the office – a sense of duty to public service ideals, or a belief in the value of the organization. The study's contrast of public- and private-sector employees was designed to isolate whether or not financial considerations were the key driver for pursuing extra work. The case against this seems overwhelmingly proven. Whatever the socially directed intentions of professionals, the aestheticization, intensification, and individualization of knowledge work through mobile devices each pose particular challenges. The unprecedented intimacy of work in the minds, laps, and pockets of information workers, combined with the management masterstroke of decentralized team-based offices, is a highly potent and coercive mode of social engagement. Any financial rewards are an added bonus.

New media scholarship has been surprisingly reticent in investigating the use of online platforms and devices for work purposes. Of the studies that do exist, even fewer identify academics' own complicity in the work-focused job market that communication technologies often facilitate. There are methodological as much as professional reasons for this. The rate of change in workplaces dependent on communication technologies poses problems for researchers seeking to monitor the use of particular platforms or packages, as do university ethics guidelines that describe the workplace and the home as two of the most sensitive locations to conduct research. For employees whose main currency is time, it is the basic inconvenience and difficulty of scheduling face-to-face interviews that is one of the greatest challenges. Matters of commercial sensitivity and the potential for management intervention also affect research ambitions in different ways. Employees who are already under pressure naturally feel constrained in how much they are willing to reveal about their job and accompanying efforts to manage it.

But perhaps the most significant obstacle this study has shown to be part of the new frontier of mobile and out-of-office work is that employees themselves rarely "count" as work the practices of message monitoring and email checking that are fundamental requirements of professional life. The need for more empirical evidence of such discounted labor practices is crucial, since the benchmark accounts of middle-class work and home life describe a period before online technologies became so thoroughly mainstream.[1] We have moved beyond the situation Hochschild described, in *The Managed Heart*, where "seeming to love the job" is a major form of emotional labor. The "deep acting" she noticed in service-industry workers bears relevance to the simulated friendships encouraged in several office cultures described in this book. But other stories prompt us to ask whether workers really are acting when they say that they love their job.

Some final comments from interviews offer useful grounds for conclusion. According to library officer Tanya, work and home life today summoned "the feeling of having a million deadlines." Her calendar was "absolutely essential" to cope with "all my home deadlines and the kids' deadlines, and school ones . . . your head starts spinning." In her view, "the whole work culture . . . has just changed dramatically in the last couple of years, and there's a lot more expected of you in terms of workload." Television producer Wendy had a particular problem with email, claiming: "the volume of it is far too great, and I find myself in physical pain sometimes, just dealing – trapped at a desk, dealing with this mass of material all day long." Wendy was concerned that online work cultures were encouraging "adverse health outcomes, because you have people tensed and hunched – sitting like this all day long. And I'm conscious of that, and sometimes resentful of this welter of stuff that is coming at me, that I have to deal with, and it's giving me a pain in my back." Project officer Jenny "spent three days having absolute anxiety about being offline" when she took a bushwalking holiday in the island state of Tasmania. Removed from her usual routine "was like coming down" from some kind of narcotic as she realized there was "no possible way I could check my email." It was hardly surprising that Jenny hadn't taken a holiday without technology since starting her job at the library.

These stories highlight the need for organizations to take greater responsibility in redefining workloads given the cultures that have developed around online communication. Initial failures to prepare workers for the escalating demands of computer-mediated jobs have only accumulated further ongoing effects as technology use is now ingrained. Managers appear uninterested in exploring how work requests might be contained, and work practices streamlined, through the informed adoption of new technology. Instead, the priorities of speed, efficiency, and economics remain at the forefront of considerations. A constant onslaught of software and platform innovations, the bulk of which must be learned in employees' own time, places the onus on individuals to keep step with the function creep affecting their jobs. On a daily basis, the widespread, institutionalized dependence on email stands at the pinnacle of the problems that knowledge workers currently suffer.

With that said, this book has also shown the extent to which workers themselves share the blame for the heightened intensity and intimacy of work. As Library Director Barbara put it: "I see people who – the phone rings and they bloody leap off a tall building to answer it or something, and I just think, get a life, they'll ring back. Nothing's that important." Barbara's attitude is a refreshing antidote to some of the material shared in these pages, where a sense of perspective regarding work obligations seemed to be missing. One of the more remarkable stories in the three years of this project was the time Miranda described a motorbike accident that took place the day before an important presentation at the office. When her husband arrived at the emergency ward to see her semi-conscious, Miranda told him: "You've got to call Holly and tell her that I might not make it in tomorrow to give the presentation . . . but bring my laptop in tomorrow and I'll be able to get it to her for Tuesday." While Miranda laughed about this afterwards ("I think it was the smack in the head from the big metal pole that was having an effect"), her panicked reaction was part of a wider pattern of behavior which included working while on sick leave and even on holiday. Defending this, she claimed to be like a lot of other people she knew these days who seemed unable to "know when to stop."

Miranda's example illustrates the difficulty faced by employees trying to establish limits to work when technology makes it constantly possible. For the middle-class professionals this book has described, feelings of responsibility and anxiety are the "anticipatory affects" of the information work- and life-style. Checking email, monitoring phones, and maintaining online awareness are the symptoms of professional presence bleed. This is the condition emerging from a workplace no longer governed by "clock time" but by the unpredictable schedule of rolling "events" (Adkins 2009). Online technologies are a key factor in making today's jobs feel variously invasive, compelling, consuming, readily available, anxiety provoking, addictive . . . and even the source of solace. Many of these qualities can be taken as the territory for passion, love, and intimacy, and it is these analogies that warrant further exploration as the necessary basis for an affective labor politics.

A labor politics of love

In a commencement address delivered at Stanford University in 2005, Steve Jobs told assembled graduates that he was lucky to have found what he loved to do early in life. Sharing the tips that led to his phenomenal rise out of the garage and into major market success on the back of the Apple brand, his talk had a clear message:

> the only way to do great work is to love what you do. If you haven't found it yet, keep looking. Don't settle. As with all matters of the heart, you'll know when you find it. And, like any great relationship, it just gets better and better as the years roll on. So keep looking until you find it. Don't settle.

Even as Jobs went on to describe the challenge of being sidelined by the company he founded at age 30, the language of love captured his sensibility: "I had been rejected, but I was still in love. And so I decided to start over." Jobs maintained that "the only thing that kept me going" during his period in the wilderness "was that I loved what I did." So to graduates he urged:

> You've got to find what you love. And that is as true for your work as it is for your lovers. Your work is going to fill a large part of your life, and the only way to be truly satisfied is to do what you believe is great work. (Jobs 2005)

Jobs's address offers a neat synopsis of the particular labor landscape described in this book. It captures the ambition, dedication, and commitment of an aspiring professional class that seeks ultimate fulfillment and passion in creative work. The language of intimacy is central to this career project. Over the past two decades, IT hardware manufacturers have made fortunes selling products through an association with the fantasy of satisfying, challenging work. This fantasy, which can only be regarded as a "romantic vision" (Armstrong 2003) of the present post-feminist workplace, is a troubling form of freedom. When iPads and smartphones function as the utopian signifiers of what it means to live the good life, freedom no longer entails liberation from labor. It is rather to be found in the recognition and release of personal productivity in an ever growing number of locations, with technology a mere conduit.

As images of these devices continue to invade public spaces and airwaves, their middle-class address should not go unnoticed. In an ostensibly global knowledge economy, the expectations and desires these images promote are far from equally distributed. As Barbara Ehrenreich warns, "the cultural ubiquity of the professional middle class" poses a challenge for critical analysis: "Nameless, and camouflaged by a culture in which it both stars and writes the scripts," the middle class sets the terms for mainstream politics, including labor politics. Rarely do academics or other cultural critics see themselves as one demographic among others, "as a class with its own peculiar assumptions and anxieties" (Ehrenreich 1990: 6).

Workers in information professions reinscribe an already substantial digital divide in a society that increasingly pivots on the distinction between information "haves" and "have-less" (Qiu 2009). The choice to engage in long hours of sacrificial labor in generally enjoyable jobs stands in stark contrast to the forms of coercion and surveillance suffered by many of the world's poorest workers. These include the legions of employees whose job it is to assemble the devices that deliver so-called flexibility to the wealthy workers of the West. A spate of worker suicides and industrial unrest in the factories of Taiwan and southern China took place as this book went to press, indicating growing dissatisfaction among second-generation migrant workers in high-tech assembly plants, among others. In this context, labor politics can be effectively understood by drawing on Jobs's analogy, as the conflicting constraints, freedoms, and opportunities of the "lovers" as opposed to the "loveless."

It is hardly incidental that by 2010, BlackBerry appeared to have taken Jobs's lessons quite literally in designing its latest ad campaign. The slogan "Love what you do" appeared in weekend magazines, in the sidebar of online networking sites, and on billboards around inner-city neighborhoods throughout the first half of the year. Around campus, arty posters bursting with images of carefree youth encouraged students to visit the "Love Shack" during orientation week to sign up for BlackBerry plans with the start of the semester. Calendars, email, Facebook, and phone could now be at hand through lectures and lunchtimes. Indeed, the number of students already using smartphones in class was a sign of how established online culture had become. These students are well on their way to leading on-call lifestyles, and for those that aren't, a whole apparatus of cultural incentives encourages them to do so in the course of their corporatized education. In such an environment, educators must be vigilant in how they encourage students not only in the take-up of coercive social media applications but also in joining an employment market that requires substantial amounts of discounted and affective labor. At the same time, students would benefit from more exposure to the large majority in a global knowledge economy for whom the prospect of fulfilling work remains "a bad joke" (Gorz 1994: 46). Aspiring professionals and educators with the opportunity to deploy cultural capital to secure both income and status have a particular responsibility to be self-reflexive about their own labor practices. This includes considering how we as individuals contribute to the hyper-competitiveness that surrounds those "rare stable jobs offering access to a career ladder" and other associated benefits of "stable, full-time, year-round employment throughout an entire lifetime" (ibid.).

Describing the impact of the BlackBerry in 2006 – just before the iPhone changed mobile computing for keeps – Research in Motion's John Balsillie explained his bestselling devices as "latency eliminators." According to this logic, Balsillie argued, "successful companies have hearts . . . and intrinsic force that makes the whole greater than the sum of its parts. BlackBerries . . . allow those hearts to beat faster" (in Connors 2006). At a time when the most profitable companies were preparing to hand out multi-million dollar handshakes to CEOs who left a trail of retrenched workers in their wake, one could be forgiven for being skeptical about Balsillie's choice of imagery. The language of love may help to explain the market triumph of his product, but this book enables us to identify some of the real-life "latencies" that smartphones help to eliminate. These include time spent with children, grocery shopping, leaving the house, even sleep. The hearts of employees may be beating faster in the wake of mobile technologies, but it is questionable whether this is with care, affection, or friendship. In many cases, it is in anticipation of the next work-related demand and the next productivity innovation imposed by management.

A labor politics of love must fight this corporatization of intimacy. It must look for visions that advance "the production of the common and the production of social life" and avoid love's foreclosure in the institutions of capital (Hardt and Negri 2009: xxii). In closing this study, I remain optimistic that new media technologies offer some of the most likely avenues for this kind of politics in future. The proliferation of online social networks and applications are a key means by which individuals are challenging the "corruption" of love at the hands of the state, the corporation, and the family (Hardt and Negri 2009). But workers must be wary of the extent to which they allow employers to exploit the bleed between personal and professional aspiration, thereby removing the bases for other intimacies.

As this research was coming to an end, Hollywood heavyweight George Clooney was receiving widespread acclaim playing the character of Ryan Bingham in the Jason Reitman film, *Up in the Air* (2009). The film opened with a close-up shot of a hostile white-collar worker addressing the camera: "This is what I get for 30 years of service to my company?" The film had an eerie synergy in its content and release date in the midst of the global financial crisis. As a professional job terminator, Clooney's Bingham is very much the nemesis of Whyte's "organization man." His motivational talks on the public speaker circuit encourage tired middle managers to empty their metaphorical backpacks. "Make no mistake," Bingham warns. "Moving is living. Your relationships are the heaviest components of your life." Bingham's character stands as the epitome of the city-hopping frequent flyer. He feels most at home when on the road, in transit, traveling to meet a never-ending list of company retrenchments. In deliberate contrast to the warmth of love and family, Bingham rejects conventional forms of intimacy. It is the "systemized friendly touches" of strangers that keeps his world "in orbit."

Fittingly for the concerns of this book, the dramatic arc of *Up in the Air* is based on the looming introduction of a technical innovation that will transform Bingham's life forever. A young hotshot business graduate finds favor upon joining the firm when she suggests that webcams would make job terminations easier and more cost-efficient in future. The imminent roll-out of this convenient online technology threatens to put an end to Bingham's pleasantly rootless existence as a citizen of the air. The trauma he experiences when faced with the prospect of coming home from a life on the road is the film's critique of the long hours cultures glamorized in so many new media marketing campaigns mentioned in previous chapters.

While he maintains a healthy ambivalence to the organization that employs him, Bingham does make one pivotal mistake in his efforts to remain unattached. Like the other white-collar workers in the film, his obsession with loyalty cards and air miles operates on the presumption that investment will have its rewards. When he reaches his coveted points total, Bingham is congratulated in person by the flight captain, who reiterates: "We really appreciate your loyalty." But by this stage in the narrative Bingham has been distracted by the thought of a woman he has loved and lost. Having spent years dreaming of the captain's handshake as his crowning career achievement, it is his failed chance for romance that renders Bingham speechless. He finds himself in the same shoes as every other worker he has counseled during his career: puzzled by the amount of faith he placed in the system, and realizing that his energies may have been better spent elsewhere.

The register of intimacy is one of the better ways to explain the process by which the white-collar workplace exploits the pact between emotional and temporal investment (see also Illouz 2007). Loyalty is the term we have used to describe this form of commitment until now, with labor politics pivoting on the demand that workers be rewarded for their devotion and monogamy. As Laura Kipnis (2003) has argued, it is surprising just how easily the language of the factory has come to inflect and shape the language of love. But a more critical language for intimacy allows us to explain what has been lost in the relationships governing employers and employees in the consuming work cultures of the present. In the closing moments of *Up in the Air*, Bingham's narration reconciles his role as a specter, transcending sanctioned forms of intimacy in his commitment to a life defined by work. Taking off on another lonely flight, he urges the audience to see the wing tip of his plane as just another star in the night sky, looking down omnisciently from on high. The image has an ethereal quality, suggesting a kind of death. It brings to mind the story we might tell a child of what happens when a relative passes away. For Bingham, and for a number of workers in this book, children, lovers and family are some of the intimate others that come and go in a larger narrative of achievement. His distant star is an image of transience, disconnection, and melancholy. It appeals to our sense of resignation that this is what a hyper-mobile modern life necessarily entails. It is an image that can be overcome.

Notes

Introduction: Work's Intimacy – Performing
Professionalism Online and On the Job

1   I am grateful for conversations with Andrew Ross that helped me
    think through these distinctions, and their attendant impact on city
    space.
2   The social and cultural capital associated with Internet use is dis-
    cussed in more detail in chapter 5. In Australia, figures for broadband
    subscriptions consistently show education and wealth to be key indica-
    tors for online connectivity, followed by the presence of children in
    the household (Osborne 2009). Responding to this data, advertising
    for the nation's largest Internet service provider during the course of
    this study played on middle-class aspirations for quality education for
    children. In the highly successful Bigpond "Rabbits" campaign, for
    instance, a child asks his father why the Great Wall of China was
    built. Not knowing the answer, Dad replies: "to keep the rabbits out."
    Playing on parental guilt, the advertisement effectively implies that
    kids will be left behind in their studies without access to the Internet.
    An overview of the campaign and others marketing Telstra products
    during the period is available on the website of Sydney's Belgiovane
    Williams McKay: <http://www.bwm.com.au/#/caseStudies>.
3   Affective labor, sometimes also referred to as immaterial labor,
    describes work with an emotional, communicative, or symbolic
    dimension. In post-Marxist theory, it is used to explain emerging
    forms of exchange value that replace the traditional idea of manual
    labor for a wage (see especially Hardt 1999; Lazzarato 1996). As
    Alan Liu (2004: 123) explains, the expression "service with a smile"

captures the sense in which many of today's jobs provide feeling or sentiment as the basis for monetary exchange. Arlie Hochschild's (1983) study of airline flight hostesses is one of the earliest examples of research into "emotional labor," and a growing literature shows its relevance to a range of industries: see, for example, Ouellette (forthcoming); Hearn (2010); Hesmondhalgh and Baker (2008); Dowling, Nunes, and Trott (2007).

4 As this book goes to print, surveys are indicating a growing backlash among employees dissatisfied with their treatment during the 2008 economic downturn, with companies also lamenting the dearth of talent and institutional memory resulting from overzealous job cuts (Stirling 2010).

5 Exceptions to this trend include Rosalind Gill and Angela McRobbie, who combine attention to work issues with a critique of the wider culture of "post-feminism." See McRobbie (2009, 2007, 2002) and Gill (2007a, 2007b).

6 The consequences of this are significant for feminism, since there is a marked division between professional experiences of work and other kinds. The distinction between unsatisfying and repetitive "McJobs" and more desirable creative and flexible "mac jobs" has long been noted, and salaried feminists in the West are certainly implicated when their flexible working conditions depend on local service industries and assembly-line manufacturing further afield. I return to these issues in conclusion, but for more on the global division of labor between women, see Ehrenreich and Hochschild (2004); Gregg (2008); Sassen (2006); Andrijasevic and Anderson (2009).

7 In late 2009, *The Internet as Playground and Factory* conference held at the New School, New York, was one of the first concerted attempts to theorize the work conditions emerging in digital and online industries. See <http://digitallabor.org/> for a list of speakers, topics, and presentations (accessed September 6, 2010). Organizers sought to identify the political stakeholders in an era of "playbour" (Kücklich 2005), building on the pioneering work of Ross (2003) and Terranova (2004) in particular. The urban US context for these discussions is far from incidental. One purpose of the present book is to show that the visions driving the most avant-garde workplaces can have much more mainstream effects.

8 An exception in media studies is Alison Hearn (2008), who places online social networking and its entrepreneurial qualities in the longer history I am citing.

9 While bookstores routinely shelve titles directed to a female audience in the "self-help" category, books offering similar kinds of advice (confidence building, improving communication and people-pleasing skills) whose target audience is male tend to appear in "business" sections. The target address for "business" as opposed to "lifestyle" supplements in major newspapers is a further instance of this casual epistemological maneuver. Recent arguments that capitalist work-

places increasingly require so-called "feminine" skills in communication (Illouz 2007; Hardt and Negri 2009) unsettle these distinctions between market and non-market based rewards for intimacy. But if women's literacy in intimacy is gaining mainstream recognition, it is only in the wider context this book describes, which is the drive to profit from friendship.

10 This is where information work has its clearest corollary with so-called "creative" work, to the extent that we may speculate whether such distinctions are entirely useful in discussions of labor politics. Certainly, academic labor shares all of these qualities described by Boltanski and Chiapello, reinforcing Ross's (2004) suggestion that scholars' sacrificial labor has been a useful business model for discounted, self-regulated labor.

Chapter 1   Selling the Flexible Workplace: The Creative Economy and New Media Fetishism

1 A 2003 report from the Queensland Government's Department of State Development and Industry anticipates these changes and captures the enthusiasm of the period. "Creativity is Big Business" is available for download at the Arts Queensland website, along with a "Creative Business Toolbox" for entrepreneurs seeking step-by-step templates for budgeting, marketing, and risk management: <http://www.arts.qld.gov.au/publications/resources/index.html> (accessed 20 September, 2010). An interesting postscript for this moment of intense policy aspiration is offered in Glover (2010).

2 The city council website explains the Living in Brisbane 2026 campaign responds to pressures such as: "more people calling Brisbane home"; "fuel prices continuing to fluctuate"; "climate change being an unprecedented global challenge"; and "skill shortages being experienced across many industries." The "vision themes" for the campaign included transforming Brisbane to a: "friendly, safe city"; "smart, prosperous city"; "clean, green city"; "active, healthy city"; "well-designed, subtropical city"; and "regional and world city." Key to my interests here, were the aspirations for a "vibrant, creative city" and "accessible, connected city": <http://www.brisbane.qld.gov.au/BCC:BASE::pc=PC_215> (accessed 13 May, 2009).

3 Aitken is quoted by Mark Ludlow, author of these comments, in "Brisbane Works on its Image," *The Weekend Australian Financial Review*, 9–13 April, p. 12. In the period captured by this study, Ludlow regularly finished columns on Brisbane's economic progress with a similar knock-out punch, a trend that is itself symbolic of the disdain held for the city in Australia's other financial centers of Sydney and Melbourne. Another concluded: "But the more things change in Queensland, the more they stay the same. On the website of C'est Bon, an upmarket French restaurant in South Brisbane, there is a reminder

for residents who may have been left behind in the city's wealth explosion: 'Attire – shoes and shirts must be worn at all times'" (Marj Ludlow and Michelle Singer, "Prices, Too, are Heading North," *The Weekend Australian Financial Review*, 17–18 January, 2009, p. 6).

4 This chapter was written prior to the devastating floods that damaged significant amounts of Brisbane's civic infrastructure in January 2011. This momentous event threatened the city's ongoing prosperity still further, even while it appeared to resurrect the popularity of the Premier.

5 As part of the strategy, number plates for registered vehicles even changed to allow residents to choose the new "Smart State" slogan on their car, replacing the more traditional branding of Queensland as "The Sunshine State."

6 Now also a successful book by Andrew Stafford, and the basis upon which the Queensland Musical Festival held an all-day concert in 2007, paying tribute to the underground punk bands of the era. Patrons attending on the day commented on the absurdity and even hypocrisy of state-sanctioned support for such an event when violence perpetuated by authorities had prevented so much of the music being performed in its original context. For these long-term residents, the wounds inflicted by the former regime had not healed in line with the city's new outlook. At the Centre for Critical and Cultural Studies at the University of Queensland, I helped organize a symposium the day before the concert where many of the musicians and activists of the time assembled to talk and reflect. Rock critic Clinton Walker noted the difference between the corporate venue of the present day and his memories from decades past: "It's great to be back at UQ. I used to come here often. To buy drugs." Full audio of the event is available at: <http://homecookedtheory.com/archives/2008/10/10/farewell-to-pig-city/>.

7 The cover story for the *Career One* lift-out in January 2008 ran with the slogan, while the feature, "Offices Head North" claimed "companies are lining up to call Brisbane home" (Tonya Turner, 26 January, 2008, pp. 6–7).

8 Richard Branson's decision to base his Virgin aircraft fleet in Brisbane can be seen as an early coup in this protracted history, generating an aura of business confidence that would continue through the decade. See Taylor (2000a, 2000b).

9 Brisbane marketing spreads in the national press in 2007 included the tag line "There's nothing to do in Brisbane" as a nod to previous stereotypes of the city; followed by "If that's what you want to do" in brackets. This was to capture two potential markets: those aspiring to enjoy the "Loud and Proud" image of the newly unleashed inner-city night-time economy and those still seeking the affordances of a subtropical climate and the slower pace of bayside living.

10 By contrast, the gay press documented a steady increase in verbal and physical violence that came with larger, transient crowds. A total

indoor smoking ban combined with a 3 a.m. "lockout policy" (to prevent venue hopping and street violence) actually contributed to large numbers of inebriated youth congregating in open space. For an account of similar law-and-order policing in the Sydney context, and the knock-on effects for gay populations, see Race (forthcoming).

11 This section draws from writing previously published in Gregg (2007).

12 In her satirical coverage of the "Walkstation," a new product that combined a treadmill with a computer workstation in airline departure lounges, Kerrie Murphy (2008) voiced her resistance to its presumption of an always-on worker: "The problem in being able to work anywhere is that we now have to work everywhere."

13 Telstra took particular interest in courting a professional female demographic in its marketing of 2007–9. In an industry setting, the company's National Business Women's Awards were a striking example of this trend. Women were depicted engaging in laptop-enabled work in a range of locations, with quotes from famous women such as Eleanor Roosevelt. "The future belongs to those who believe in the beauty of their dreams" was one such caption attached to a female worker waiting for a plane and working on her notebook.

14 David Flynn's (2006) "Don't Commute" column in the aptly titled "Hype" section of the *Sydney Morning Herald*'s *Icon* was the most striking example of advertising passing as copy during this period. The story explains how "laptop leader" Toshiba is leading the way in adopting flexible working practices, and even provides a link to the Toshiba website for readers to download a list of guidelines and resources for personal use. See also Simon Tsang's step-by-step guide to Gmail in "Soothe the Savage Inbox" (Tsang 2008), *The Bulletin*'s Business IT "Wireless and IP Special" (2005); "A Guide to Pocket Offices," *Sydney Morning Herald Icon*, June 3, 2006. In Brisbane's *Courier-Mail*, Stephen Fenech (2007) provides an overview of Lexmark wireless printers having "traveled to Lexington, Kentucky, as a guest of Lexmark."

15 *The Sydney Morning Herald*'s "Essential Guides" series of 2005, available free to readers, included pamphlets on "The Workplace" and "How to Efficiently Run Your Home Office" (the latter was sponsored by Telstra, the nation's largest telecommunications provider).

16 See O'Connor (2008); Henry Budd, "Influenced by the Inbox," *The Courier-Mail*, Career One, October 20–1, 2007; Henry Budd, "Ergonomic Employment," *The Courier-Mail*, Career One, May 10–11, 2008, p. 9; Emma Connors, "Checking Email is Now a Scourge of the Workplace," *Australian Financial Review*, June 3, 2005; Kate Mackenzie, "The Rise and Rise of a Killer Application," *The Australian*, IT Business, April 18, 2006, p. 4.

17 See Mann's website at <http://www.43folders.com/>. A sample of business self-help gleaned from a second-hand book fair in Brisbane during this study shows that this is hardly a new phenomenon: see

Collis and LeBoeuf (1995); LeBoeuf (1979); Cole (2001); Adair (1982); Mackenzie (1972); Bernard (1991); Morgenstern (2001); and Bliss (1991). The latter had clear resonances and at times word-for-word overlap in sections of another breakout motivational business text in the period of analysis, *The 4-Hour Work Week* (Ferriss 2007).

Chapter 2 Working from Home: The Mobile Office and the Seduction of Convenience

1 Karl Marx, *Economic and Philosophic Manuscripts 1844*, edited with an introduction by Dirk J. Struik; translated by Martin Milligan (Lawrence & Wishart, 1973), pp. 110–11.
2 Consider the following sample of academic studies: Haddon and Silverstone (1993); Frolick et al. (1993); Hill et al. (1998); Bentley and Yoong (2000); Taskin and Devos (2005); Tremblay et al. (2006); Gajendran and Harrison (2007).
3 I discuss the Australian policy context in more detail in "The Normalisation of Flexible Female Labour in the Information Economy" (Gregg 2008), and "Do Your Homework: New Media, Old Problems" (Gregg 2011).
4 I mention television here to suggest one of several links between this study and the findings of Robert Putnam's *Bowling Alone* (2000). Putnam provides "powerful" if "circumstantial" evidence that television watching coincided with "the national decline in social connectedness" in the United States. Those who relied most heavily on televised entertainment were also those "most likely to have dropped out of civic and social life – who spent less time with friends, were less involved in community organizations, and were less likely to participate in public affairs" (2000: 246). While I have much happier things to say about television, I share Putnam's wider interest in understanding the decline in civic and social life, including the role of the workplace in offering replacements for other forms of community.
5 "I am significantly more productive as I do not have as many interruptions" says Amanda Farmer, account manager for a PR firm in Waco, Texas, in Marilyn Gardner, "Your Place of Business," *The Courier-Mail*, Career One, Saturday, January 12, 2008.

Chapter 3 Part-time Precarity: Discount Labor and Contract Careers

1 At the time I write this book, casual appointments comprise over 50 percent of the teaching load of Australian universities, which is to say that Angela and Vince are representative of academic employment

more broadly. Union-led campaigns to force universities to reveal the percentage of casually employed staff were major features of the industrial landscape in the years of the study. The title for this section, "smart casuals," is taken from one such campaign, and is part of a number of initiatives seeking to improve the conditions for junior scholars. See Gregg (2009b).

2   The situation for international students in Australia, one of many countries now heavily invested in the booming global economy in higher education, is another matter again, and is discussed with typical prescience in Neilson (2009).

3   In one example he mentioned, Patrick would regularly "borrow" his colleagues' chairs when he needed to sit down, since he didn't have a dedicated workspace of his own. This action would upset his co-workers when they found their chair missing – a reaction he saw as overly obsessive about mere symbols of office status.

Chapter 4   To CC: Or Not to CC: Teamwork in Office Culture

1   Amply demonstrated in the phenomenal success of motivational texts like *Who Moved My Cheese?* (Johnson 1998). Beyond corporate workplaces, a glance at university staff development offerings at my own university includes courses on "living with change" as part of a desirable skill set for employees.

2   Thanks to Nadia Mizner for her foresight in taking photos of the posters described in this section.

3   The period 2008–9 saw a 60 percent surge in complaints to the Telecommunications Industry Ombudsman in Australia. An amount of 481,418 registered cases equated to a rate of 1,850 every weekday, or nearly four complaints a minute (Bita 2010a, 2010b).

4   The beach scene follows the examples raised in chapter 1 depicting "freedom" from work with mobile technology. In these images, the beach serves as a utopian – literally empty – signifier, as I discuss in more detail in Gregg (2007).

5   The telco was a major proponent of individually negotiated, non-union contract labor during the brief period of "Work Choices" indus-trial regulation in Australia. This legislation, which placed the onus on workers to engage in direct discussion with employers to set the terms of their employment, faced a highly successful union-led cam-paign during the 2007 Federal Election campaign that significantly contributed to the Labor Party's subsequent victory. At the time of writing, the telco's announcement to sack 900 frontline staff in 2010, including 300 workers in senior management, has been met with ambivalence by unions: "I don't think there will be a lot of sympathy from the [telco's] employees for the managers who have been cutting staff themselves over the last decade," one representative of the

Victorian Communications, Electrical, Plumbing and Electrical Union (CEPU) remarked (AAP 2010a).

6 I discuss office toilets and other spaces of reprieve from the performance of corporate cool in Gregg (2010a).

7 Rachael King (2008) describes the challenge faced by large companies like IBM, which hired 20,000 new staff in 2007 alone, in generating shared values: "When the company can't get recent hires to mingle in person, it has them interact virtually, using the same kind of 3D technology that runs virtual worlds such as Linden Lab's Second Life." In the same article, Nicole Yankelovich, from Sun Microsystems' social media labs, says "Virtual world technology is a way to bring the company together to build a global corporate culture where people are on equal footing." Yet it is unclear how such initiatives would appeal to workers like Sam or Richard, or how smaller-scale organizations could hope to deal with these changes with fewer resources.

8 The trend among freelance workers and start-up entrepreneurs to rent shared office space or work from cafes suggests that the isolation of working independently at home isn't for everyone (see Gaylord 2008).

9 In response to a presentation of this research at Melbourne University in 2008, an audience member observed that employees in my study betrayed the affective symptoms of a "post-nicotine" workplace. The relationship between white-collar work and a range of drug consumption practices would certainly be an excellent basis for further studies.

Chapter 5   Facebook Friends: Security Blankets and Career Mobility

1 The accompanying text for the ad captures some of the wider conditions surrounding this chapter and the book as a whole: "These days it seems we have less and less time to chat. Yet, in the middle of this time crunch we still find hours and hours for things like social networking sites. There's nothing wrong with that, just don't forget to spare a little time to phone home. It's one of the few pleasures that won't break your budget in challenging times."

2 Wilson (2007) and Boyd (2009) discuss class and age differences amongst MySpace and Facebook users, while Hjorth's (2009) study of social media platforms in Singapore, Korea, Hong Kong, and Tokyo is an important contrast to the anglocentrism of much social media commentary.

3 This is different from claiming that social media are inherently narcissistic. Joanna Zylinska (2009) highlights the productive dimensions to the self-monitoring behavior encouraged by social networking sites, with reference to both Levinas and a Foucauldian ethics of "care of the self." Her critical perspective is a useful contrast to the many

scholars investigating the rise of social networking sites on the assumption that the narcissism of online platforms is innate, obvious, and appalling. Cohen (2006) offers another excellent exception.

4   Bourdieu deploys "elective affinities" from the work of Max Weber, who used the term to explain the apparent "chemistry" of well-suited couples and the social function of marriage, as well as the relationship between Calvinism and Capitalism in his most famous work, *The Protestant Ethic and the Spirit of Capitalism* (1930). See Howe (1978).

5   Personal information on profile pages is also the major repository for targeted advertising, Facebook's main revenue source, and a growing focus for critical scholarly attention. Mark Andrejevic (2007) has anticipated many of these trends in his ongoing research into the surveillance properties of interactive media.

6   Here it is worth remembering that as a part-time musician in a relatively small city, Patrick saw little hope in having an audience for his shows beyond his actually existing friends and acquaintances. For an extended discussion of pro-am practices in the Brisbane music scene during the period of the study, see Rogers (2011).

7   The limitations of new media accounts of online social networking, which consistently fetishize youth users, are discussed in Driscoll and Gregg (2008a, 2008b).

8   My own students gave examples of employers demanding to be Facebook friends, and potential employers asking for profile printouts prior to interviews, in 2009 classes. The comments section on a subsequent blogpost offers interesting insight into the legalities of the situation; see Gregg (2009c). In 2010, high-profile Australian Olympian swimmer Stephanie Rice faced intense media scrutiny for derogatory comments made in the heat of the moment on Twitter, leading to a number of sponsors pulling lucrative contracts with the star (Robertson 2010). This embarrassing fate was a portent of the kind of backlash that may become more common for other workers in light of the trends discussed in this book. The ironic twist to the Rice story was that her stratospheric rise to public prominence and celebrity was facilitated by risqué photographs leaked to the media from her Facebook profile page just a few years earlier.

9   An anonymous reader of this book's proposal suggested this argument, for which I am grateful.

10   As this book goes to press, David Fincher's *The Social Network* is set for global release, which may pose the biggest challenge to date for site founder, Mark Zuckerberg. The film trailer carried a quote that captured the appeal of the Facebook concept: "We're talking about taking the whole social experience of college and putting it online." The film made the demographic presumed for the site abundantly clear, while its portrayal of Zuckerberg as an outsider hoping to join the ranks of the wealthy elite reinforced the wider cultural appetite for class mobility suggested in this chapter. In the same month, Zuckerberg took 35th place in the latest Forbes Rich List, and *Vanity*

Fair magazine named him at the top of its annual New Establishment list (Sherwell 2010) – a status update of considerable proportions.

Chapter 6 Know Your Product: Online Branding and the Evacuation of Friendship

1 The title for this chapter, "Know Your Product," is a reference to the song by standout Brisbane punk band of the 1970s, The Saints. The scathing anthem written to rebuke the commercially minded music industry has relevance to the creative workers in this book who were encouraged to develop a winning formula for success – on the one hand, to capture the lucrative youth market, on the other, to withstand the vulnerabilities brought by the recession. During the study, The Saints re-formed for a special event concert to mark Brisbane's new-found status as a world leader in producing rock talent for export; see chapter 1, fn. 6.

2 The number of titles that could be named here is potentially infinite, and these references are merely illustrative. However, the breathless speed of this publishing genre is captured better than most in Geoff Livingstone's 2007 title, *Now Is Gone: A Primer on New Media for Executives and Entrepreneurs*. As Kevin Rose, university drop-out and founder of digg.com, remarked in a *Businessweek* cover story from late 2008: "Things change in the shower in the morning" (Hamm 2008).

3 This is without mentioning working conditions at the start-ups fueling the second dot.com boom. A *Wall Street Journal* article in May 2009 claimed Twitter users had "jumped to an estimated 32.1 million users from 1.6 million a year ago," but employee numbers were still at 45 (up from 21 in January). In keeping with the trends discussed in chapter 4, founders Evan Williams and Biz Stone were described as wanting to "develop the company slowly in order to find people who fit with its culture." This was being defined "through rituals such as family-style lunches and weekly 'teas' or happy hours." See Vascellaro (2009).

4 By 2010, the broadcaster had developed a formal social media policy, and employees struggling to fit the new paradigm faced severe reprimand. See AAP (2010).

5 In the case of the broadcaster, regular "events" for the news department (elections, bushfires, riots, or floods) placed the priority on the story over and above the worker. Meanwhile, in his role overseeing a complete overhaul of the online news site in 2008, Frank reported several all-nighters in his quest to meet management deadlines for the site relaunch. These binge periods regularly resulted in inflamed tendonitis and other physical symptoms from computer overuse.

6 The limitations of this demographic are acknowledged in Jenkins's preface to *Convergence Culture*, but the commercial thrust of the book does little to prevent the reification of such users' preferences. See Driscoll and Gregg (forthcoming) and other articles in the forthcoming special issue of *Cultural Studies* discussing Jenkins's work.

7   Pam's experience fits with other research into the changing role of librarians in an information economy. Tracy and Hyashi's (2007) study of university librarians concludes: "As libraries have come to more fully rely on technology, two fundamental shifts in library work and patron activities appear inevitable. First – and already well under-way – is the expanding number of tasks delegated to library workers. Second, what was once the public service work of the librarian will increasingly become the 'consumptive work' (search, retrieval, and reproduction via ICT) of library patrons at the library, and in their homes and workplaces" (63). McKercher and Mosco's (2007) edited collection, in which this chapter appears, and the follow-up collabora-tion, *The Laboring of Communication* (2008) are promising signs of the momentum building for critical studies of technology in the white-collar workplace, some 20 years after Zubkoff's (1988) *In the Age of the Smart Machine.*

8   Thanks to Catherine Driscoll for feedback on this chapter, and for the collaboration that developed as a result (Driscoll and Gregg forthcoming).

9   In the height of these discussions, blogger Charlene Li mused, "What's missing is marketing value based on how valuable I am in the context of my influence." This followed the remarkable claim that "in the future, social networks will be like air. They will be anywhere and everywhere we need and want them to be . . . without that social context in our connected lives, we won't really feel like we are truly living and alive, just as without sufficient air, we won't really be able to breathe deeply": <http://blogs.forrester.com/charleneli/2008/03/the-future-of-s.html>.

Chapter 7   Home Offices and Remote Parents: Family Dynamics in Online Households

1   This idyllic home network arrangement, in which wealthy families simply buy more computers to avoid conflict over Internet access, matched advertising copy of the period which sold home broadband subscriptions to Australians with the slogan "We all get on when we all get on." The metrocentric and heteronormative assumptions of this and other Telstra campaigns are analysed in Gregg (2010b).

Chapter 8   Long Hours, High Bandwidth: Negotiating Domesticity and Distance

1   This chapter was written prior to the release of Sherry Turkle's (2011) *Alone Together: Why We Expect More From Technology and Less From Each Other,* which shares similar concerns.

Chapter 9   On Call

1   Belinda's comments shed light on the difficulties Lisa mentioned, back in chapter 2, about the stress involved in her previous position in radio.
2   Seek.com.au is the largest online job portal in Australia. Continuing job cuts to middle management at the telco in the period since the study's conclusion only confirmed the sense in Miranda's wary attitude.

Conclusion: Labor Politics in an Online
Workplace – The Lovers vs. the Loveless

1   Thinking of Arlie Hochschild's work especially, but also the ground-breaking research of Christena Nippert-Eng (1996), which has recently been extended to account for online "boundary work" in Nippert-Eng (2010).

References

AAP. (2010a). Sacked Bosses Get Little Sympathy. *The Age.* July 22. <http://news.theage.com.au/breaking-news-national/sacked-bosses-get-little-sympathy-20100722-10lo0.html>; accessed September 23, 2010.

AAP. (2010b). ABC Presenter Reprimanded Over Twitter. *Sydney Morning Herald.* <http://news.smh.com.au/breaking-news-national/abc-presenter-reprimanded-over-twitter-20100820-138bp.html>; accessed September 26, 2010.

Adair, J. (1982). *Effective Time Management: How to Save Time and Spend it Wisely.* London: Pan Macmillan.

Adkins, L. (2008). From Retroactivation to Futurity: The End of the Sexual Contract. *NORA – Nordic Journal of Feminist and Gender Research* 16(3): 182–201.

Adkins, L. (2009). Presentation at Cultural Work and Creative Biographies Symposium, April 1. Milton Keynes: Open University.

Adkins, L. and Jokinen, E. (2008). Introduction: Gender, Living and Labour in the Fourth Shift. *NORA – Nordic Journal of Feminist and Gender Research,* 16(3): 138–49.

Agamben, G. (2005). *State of Exception.* Chicago, IL: University of Chicago Press.

Allon, F. (2008). *Renovation Nation: Our Obsession with Home.* Sydney: University of New South Wales Press.

Amman, J., Carpenter, T., and Neff, G. (eds) (2007). *Surviving the New Economy.* Boulder, CO: Paradigm Publishers.

Anderson, C. (2004). The Long Tail. *Wired* 12(10) (October). <http://www.wired.com/wired/archive/12.10/tail.html>.

Andrejevic, M. (2007). *iSpy: Surveillance and Power in the Interactive Era.* Lawrence, KA: University Press of Kansas.

Andresky-Fraser, J. (2001). *White Collar Sweatshop: The Deterioration of Work and Its Rewards in Corporate America*. New York: W.W. Norton.

Andrijasevic, R. and Anderson, B. (eds) (2009) Conflicts of Mobility: Migration, Labour and Political Subjectivities. Special Issue of *Subjectivity* 29(1) (December): 363–6.

Armstrong, J. (2003). *Conditions of Love: The Philosophy of Intimacy*. New York: W.W. Norton.

Banerjee, S. (2009). Best Buy Seeks Candidate With 250 Twitter followers. *Telegraph*. July 14. <http://www.telegraph.co.uk/technology/twitter/5825826/Best-Buy-seeks-candidate-with-250-Twitter-followers.html>.

Banks, M. (2007). *The Politics of Cultural Work*. Basingstoke: Palgrave.

Banks, M. (2009). Fit and Working Again? The Instrumental Leisure of the Creative Class. *Environment and Planning A*. 41(3): 668–81.

Barrett, M. (1980). *Women's Oppression Today: Problems in Marxist Feminist Analysis*. London: Verso and New Left Books.

Bartelby, A. (2009). FOLLOW FAIL: The Top 10 Reasons I Will Not Follow You in Return on Twitter. *Mashable: The Social Media Guide*. January 6. <http://mashable.com/2009/01/06/twitter-follow-fail/>.

Bauman, Z. (2005). *Liquid Life*. Cambridge: Polity.

Baxter, E. (2008). In Your Facebook. *Sydney Morning Herald*, The Guide. February 25. <http://www.smh.com.au/news/web/in-your-facebook/2008/02/23/ 1203467445965.html?page=fullpage>.

Benkler, Y. (2006). *The Wealth Of Networks: How Social Production Transforms Markets and Freedom*. New Haven, CT, Yale University Press.

Bentley, K. and Yoong, P. (2000). Knowledge Work and Telework: An Exploratory Study. *Internet Research*. 10(4): 346–56.

Berlant, L. (1997). *The Queen of America Goes to Washington City: Essays on Sex and Citizenship*. Durham, NC, Duke University Press.

Berlant, L. (2007). Faceless Book. *Supervalent Thought*. <http://supervalentthought.com/2007/12/25/faceless-book/>; Accessed September 26, 2010.

Berlant, L. (2008). After the Good Life, the Impasse: *Human Resources, Time Out*, and the Precarious Present. Faculty of Arts Dean's Lecture, University of Melbourne. August 13.

Bernard, M. E. (1991). *Procrastinate Later: How To Motivate Yourself To Do It Now*. Melbourne: Schwartz and Wilkinson.

Bita, N. (2010a). Time's Up for Telcos, Consumers Say. *The Australian*. September 17. <http://www.theaustralian.com.au/news/nation/times-up-for-telcos-consumers-say/story-e6frg6nf-1225925069145>; accessed September 23, 2010.

Bita, N. (2010b). Lift Your Game or We'll Force You, Ombudsman Tells Telcos. *The Australian*. September 4. <http://www.theaustralian.com.au/news/nation/lift-your-game-or-well-force-you-ombudsman-tells-telcos/story-e6frg6nf-1225914005628>; accessed September 23, 2010.

Bliss, E. C. (1991) *Getting Things Done: The ABC of Time Management*. New York: Warner. First published 1976.

Boltanski, L. and Chiapello, È. (2007/2005). *The New Spirit of Capitalism*, G. Elliott (trans). London: Verso.

Bourdieu, P. (1984). *Distinction: A Social Critique of the Judgement of Taste*, Richard Nice (trans.). Cambridge, MA: Harvard University Press.

Boyd, d. (2009). White Flight in Networked Publics? How Race and Class Shaped American Teen Engagement with MySpace and Facebook. Available at *apophenia*: <www.danah.org/papers/2009/WhiteFlightDraft3.pdf>; accessed March 23, 2010.

Brady, D. (2007). Creating Brand You. *Business Week*. August 20. <http://www.businessweek.com/magazine/content/07_34/b4047419.htm>.

Bradwell, P. and Reeves, R. (2008). *Network Citizens*. Demos Report. Available at <www.demos.co.uk/publications/networkcitizens>; accessed March 23, 2010.

Brogan, C. and Smith, J. (2009). *Trust Agents: Using the Web to Build Influence, Improve Reputation, and Earn Trust*. New Jersey: Wiley & Sons.

Brophy, E. and de Peuter, G. (2007). Immaterial Labor, Precarity, and Recomposition. In Mosco, V. and McKercher, C. (eds), *Knowledge Workers in the Information Society*. Lanham, MD: Lexington Books, pp. 177–91.

Bruns, A. (2008). *Blogs, Wikipedia, Second Life, and Beyond: From Production to Produsage*. New York: Peter Lang.

Budd, H. (2007). Influenced by the Inbox. *The Courier-Mail*, Career One, October 20–1.

Budd, H. (2008). Ergonomic Employment. *The Courier-Mail*, Career One, May 10–11.

The Bulletin. (2005). Business IT "Wireless and IP Special," March 15: 52–8.

Caldwell, J. T. (2008). *Production Culture: Industrial Reflexivity and Critical Practice in Film and Television*. Durham, NC: Duke University Press.

Carr, Kim (2009). Federal Industry Minister Delivers Dire Jobs Warning Lateline, ABC Television, February 26, 2009. Available at: <http://www.abc.net.au/lateline/ content/2008/s2502600.htm>.

Castells, M. (2000). *The Information Age: Economy, Society and Culture. Volume 1: The Rise of the Network Society*. Oxford: Blackwell.

Chaney, P. (2009). *The Digital Handshake: Seven Proven Strategies to Grow Your Business Using Social Media*. New Jersey: Wiley & Sons.

Cohen, K. R. (2006). A Welcome For Blogs. *Continuum: Journal of Media and Cultural Studies* 20(2): 161–73.

Cole, K. (2001). *Make Time: Practical Time Management that Really Works!* Harlow: Pearson Education.

Collis, J. and LeBoeuf, M. (1995). *Work Smarter Not Harder*. Sydney: HarperCollins Business.

Connors, E. (2005). Checking Email is Now a Scourge of the Workplace. *Australian Financial Review*, June 3.

Connors, E. (2006). Blackchat. *Australian Financial Review Boss*, May.

Connors, E. (2008). In Search of the Small Picture. *The Weekend Australian Financial Review*, June 7–8: 28–9.

Crawford, K. (2009). These Foolish Things: On Intimacy and Insignificance in Mobile Media. In Gerard Goggin and Larissa Hjorth (eds), *Mobile Technologies: From Telecommunications to Media*. New York: Routledge, pp. 252–65.

de Botton, A. (2009). *The Pleasures and Sorrows of Work*. London: Hamish Hamilton.

de Certeau, M. (1988). *The Practice of Everyday Life*. Berkeley, Los Angeles, CA, and London: University of California Press.

Delaney, B. (2009). Flexibility Has its Flaws. *Sydney Morning Herald*, My Career, August 15–16.

Deuze, M. (2007). *Media Work*. Digital Media and Society Series. Cambridge: Polity.

Dowling, E., Nunes, R., and Trott, B. (eds) (2007). Immaterial and Affective Labour: Explored. *Ephemera* Special Issue 7(1): 1–7.

Driscoll, C. and Gregg, M. (2008a). Broadcast Yourself: Moral Panic, Youth Culture and Internet Studies. In B. Smaill and U. Rodrigues, *Youth Media in the Asia Pacific Region*. Newcastle: Cambridge Scholars Press, pp. 71–86.

Driscoll, C. and Gregg, M. (2008b). Message Me: Temporality, Location and Everyday Technologies. *Media International Australia* 128 (Special Issue on Digital Literacy): 128–36.

Driscoll, C. and Gregg, M. (2010). My Profile: The Ethics of Virtual Ethnography. *Emotion, Space and Society* 3(1) (May): 15–20.

Driscoll, C. and Gregg, M. (forthcoming). *Convergence Culture* and the Legacy of Feminist Cultural Studies. *Cultural Studies*.

The Economist (2010). All's Just Grate in a Cheesy Office. Syndicated in *The Weekend Australian Financial Review*. September 18–19.

Edwards, P. and Wajcman, J. (2005). *The Politics of Working Life*. Oxford: Oxford University Press.

Ehrenreich, B. (1990). *Fear of Falling: The Inner Life of the Middle Class*. New York: Harper Perennial.

Ehrenreich, B. and Hochschild, A. R. (2004). *Global Woman: Nannies, Maids, and Sex Workers in the New Economy*. New York: Henry Holt and Company.

Fenech, S. (2007). Printing Perfection. *Courier-Mail*, April 18.

Ferriss, T. (2007). *The 4-Hour Work Week: Escape 9–5, Live Anywhere and Join the New Rich*. New York: Crown.

Flew, T. (2010). Toward a Cultural Economic Geography of Creative Industries and Urban Development: Introduction to the Special Issue on Creative Industries and Urban Development. *The Information Society* 26(2): 85–91.

Flew, T. and Cunningham, S. (2010). Creative Industries After the First Decade of Debate. *The Information Society* 26(2): 113–23.

Flew, T., Ching, G. Stafford, A. and Tacchi, J. (2001). *Music Industry Development and Brisbane's Future as a Creative City*. Brisbane City

Council and Queensland University of Technology. Brisbane: Creative Industries Research and Applications Centre.

Florida, R. (2002). *The Rise of the Creative Class: And How It's Transforming Work, Leisure, Community and Everyday Life*. New York: Basic Books.

Flynn, D. (2006). Don't Commute. *Sydney Morning Herald,* Icon, October 21–2.

Fortunati, L. (1995). *The Arcane of Reproduction. Housework, Prostitution, Labor and Capital*. New York: Autonomedia. First published as *L'arcano della riproduzione. Casalinghe, prostitute, operai e capitale*, Padova: Marsilio, 1981.

Frolick, M. N., Wilkes, R. B. and Urwiler, R. (1993). Telecommuting as a Workplace Alternative: An Identification of Significant Factors in American Firms' Determination of Work-at-Home Policies. *Journal of Strategic Information Systems* 2: 206–22.

Gajendran, R. S. and Harrison, D. A. (2007). The Good, the Bad, and the Unknown about Telecommuting: Meta-analysis of Psychological Mediators and Individual Consequences. *Journal of Applied Psychology* 92: 152–41.

Gardner, Marilyn (2008). Your Place of Business. *Courier-Mail*. Career One, January 12.

Gaylord, C. (2008). A Home for the Lonely. *Courier-Mail*. Career One, April 5–6. Syndicated from *Christian Science Monitor*.

Gill, R. (2007a). *Gender and the Media*. Cambridge: Polity.

Gill, R. (2007b). *Technobohemians or the New Cybertariat? New Media Work in Amsterdam a Decade after the Web*. Network Notebooks 01, Amsterdam: Institute of Network Cultures.

Gill, R. and A. Pratt, (2008). In the Social Factory? Immaterial Labour, Precariousness and Cultural Work. *Theory, Culture & Society* 25(7–8): 1–30.

Glover, S. (2010). Failed Fantasies of Cohesion: Retrieving Positives from the Stalled Dream of Whole-of-Government Cultural Policy. *M/C Journal*. 13(1). <http://journal.media-culture.org.au/index.php/mcjournal/article/view/213>; accessed September 20, 2010.

Goffman, E. (1973). *The Presentation of Self in Everyday Life*. New York: The Overlook Press. First published 1959.

Gorz, A. (1994). *Capitalism, Socialism, Ecology*, trans. Chris Turner. London: Verso.

Gregg, M. (2006). *Cultural Studies' Affective Voices*. Houndsmills: Palgrave.

Gregg, M. (2007). Freedom to Work: The Impact of Wireless on Labour Politics. *Media International Australia* Special Issue on Wireless Technologies and Cultures 125 (November): 57–70.

Gregg, M. (2008). The Normalisation of Flexible Female Labour in the Information Economy. *Feminist Media Studies* 8(3): 285–99.

Gregg, M. (2009a). Banal Bohemia: Blogging from the Ivory Tower Hot-desk. *Convergence: The Journal of Research into New Media Technologies* 15(4): 470–83.

Gregg, M. (2009b). Why Academia is no Longer a Smart Choice. *New Matilda*. Available at: <http://newmatilda.com/2009/11/24/academia-no-longer-smart-choice>; accessed December 22, 2009.

Gregg, M. (2009c). Privacy and Work. *Home Cooked Theory*. August 17. <http://homecookedtheory.com/archives/2009/08/17/privacy-and-work/>; accessed September 26, 2010.

Gregg, M. (2010a). On Friday Night Drinks: Workplace Affect in the Age of the Cubicle. In Gregg, M. and Seigworth, G (eds), *The Affect Theory Reader*. Durham, NC: Duke University Press, pp. 250–67.

Gregg, M. (2010b). 'Available in Selected Metros Only': Rural Melancholy and the Promise of Online Connectivity. *Cultural Studies Review* 16(1) March.

Gregg, M. (2011, forthcoming). Do Your Homework: New Media, Old Problems. *Feminist Media Studies*.

Grossberg, L. (1997). *Dancing in Spite of Myself: Essays On Popular Culture*. Durham, NC:Duke University Press.

Haddon, L. and Silverstone, R. (1993). *Teleworking in the 1990s: A View from the Home*. Martlesham: British Telecom.

Hamm, S. (2008). Whatever Happened to Silicon Valley Innovation? *Businessweek*. December 31. <http://www.businessweek.com/magazine/content/09_02/b4115028730216.htm>.

Hardt, M. (1999). Affective Labor. *boundary 2* 26(2): 89–100.

Hardt, M. and Negri, A. (2009). *Commonwealth*. Cambridge, MA, Belknap Press of Harvard University Press.

Hay, J. (2006). Designing Homes to be the First Line of Defense: Safe Households, Mobilization, and the New Mobile Privatization. *Cultural Studies* 20(4–5): 349–77.

Hearn, A. (2008). Variations on the Branded Self: Theme, Invention, Improvisation and Inventory. In D. Hesmondhalgh and J. Toynbee (eds), *The Media and Social Theory*. London: Routledge, pp. 194–210.

Hearn, A. (2010). Reality Television, *The Hills* and the Limits of the Immaterial Labour Thesis. *tripleC – Cognition, Communication, Co-operation* 8(1).

Heffernan, V. (2009). Let Them Eat Tweets, *New York Times*, The Medium, April 17. Available at: <http://themedium.blogs.nytimes.com/2009/04/17/let-them-eat-tweets/>.

Hesmondhalgh, D. and Baker, S. (2008). Creative Work and Emotional Labour in the Television Industry. *Theory, Culture & Society* 25(7–8) (December): 97–118.

Higgs, P. and Cunningham, S. (2008). Creative Industries Mapping: Where Have We Come From and Where Are We Going? *Creative Industries Journal* 1(1): 7–30.

Hill, E. J., Miller, B. C., Weiner, S. P. and Colihan, J. (1998). Influences of the Virtual Office on Aspects of Work and Work/Life Balance. *Personnel Psychology* 51: 667–83.

Hjorth, L. (2009). *Mobile Media in the Asia-Pacific: Gender and the Art of Being Mobile*. London Routledge.

Hobson, D. (1982). *Crossroads: The Drama of a Soap Opera.* London: Methuen.

Hochschild, A. R. (1983/2003). *The Managed Heart: Commercialization of Human Feeling.* Twentieth Anniversary Edition, Berkley, CA: University of California Press.

Hochschild, A. R. (1997). *The Time Bind: When Work Becomes Home and Home Becomes Work.* New York: Metropolitan Books.

Hochschild, A. R. and Machung, A. (1989). *The Second Shift: Working Parents and the Revolution at Home.* New York: Viking.

Hoggart, R. (1957). *The Uses of Literacy.* Harmondsworth: Penguin.

Howe, R. H. (1978). Max Weber's Elective Affinities: Sociology Within the Bounds of Pure Reason. *The American Journal of Sociology* 84(2): 366–85.

Huws, U. (2003). *The Making of a Cybertariat: Collected Essays.* New York: Monthly Review Press; and London: Merlin Press.

Illouz, E. (2007). *Cold Intimacies: The Making of Emotional Capitalism.* Cambridge: Polity.

Ito, Joi. (2007). Radar. *Joi Ito's Web,* <http://joi.ito.com/archives/2007/03/14/radar.html>.

Jenkins, H. (2006). *Convergence Culture: Where Old and New Media Collide.* New York: New York University Press.

Jenkins, C. (2008). Employers Move to Curb Surge in Social Networking. *The Australian Financial Review.* February 12.

Jennings, J. (2009). Tired of Waiting. *Sydney Morning Herald,* My Career, August 15–16.

Jobs, S. (2005). "You've Got to Find What You Love," Jobs Says. *Stanford University News,* June 14. <http://news.stanford.edu/news/2005/june15/jobs-061505.html>.

Johnson, S. (1998). *Who Moved My Cheese? An Amazing Way to Deal with Change in Your Work and in Your Life.* New York: Putnam.

Keane, M. (2007). *Created in China: The Great New Leap Forward.* Abingdon and New York: Routledge.

Killen, S. (2008). Do Homework before Working from Home. *Courier-Mail,* Career One, April 5–6: 6–7.

King, R. (2008). Global Firms Move Water Cooler Online. *The Weekend Australian Financial Review.* June 7–8: 32.

Kipnis, L. (2003). *Against Love: A Polemic.* New York: Vintage.

Klaebe, H. (2006). *Sharing Stories: Problems and Potentials of Oral History and Digital Storytelling and the Writer/Producer's Role in Constructing a Public Place.* PhD Thesis. Faculty of Creative Industries, Queensland University of Technology. Available at: <http://eprints.qut.edu.au/16364/>; accessed September 20, 2010.

Kücklich, Julian (2005). Precarious Playbour: Modders and the Digital Games Industry. *Fibreculture Journal* 5. Available at: <http://five.fibreculturejournal.org/fcj-025-precarious-playbour-modders-and-the-digital-games-industry/>.

Lazzarato, M. (1996). Immaterial Labor. In P. Virno and M. Hardt (eds), *Radical Thought in Italy: A Potential Politics*. Minneapolis, MN: University of Minnesota Press, pp. 133–47.

LeBoeuf, M. (1979). *Working Smart: How to Accomplish More in Half the Time*. New York: Warner.

Levit, A. (2009). Go On, Acquire a Brand in Order to Sell Yourself. Weekend Professional Education *The Weekend Australian* May 2–3. (Reprinted from *The Wall Street Journal*.)

Li, C. and Bernoff, J. (2008). *Groundswell: Winning in a World Transformed by Social Technologies*. Boston, MA: Forrester Inc.

Liu, A. (2004). *The Laws of Cool: Knowledge Work and the Culture of Information*. Chicago, IL, and London, University of Chicago Press.

Livingstone, G. (2007). *Now Is Gone: A Primer on New Media for Executives and Entrepreneurs*. Silver Spring, MD: Bartleby.

Lovink, G. and Rossiter, N. (eds), *MyCreativity Reader: A Critique of Creative Industries*. Amsterdam: Institute of Network Cultures.

Mackenzie, A. (2008). The Affect of Efficiency: Personal Productivity Equipment Encounters the Multiple. *Ephemera: Theory and Politics in Organization* 8(2): 137–56.

Mackenzie, K. (2006). The Rise and Rise of a Killer Application. *The Australian,* IT Business, April 18.

Mackenzie, R. A. (1972). *The Time Trap: How to Get More Done in Less Time*. New York: McGraw-Hill.

McKercher, C. and Mosco, V. (eds). (2007). *Knowledge Workers in the Information Society*. Lanham, MD: Lexington Books.

McRobbie, A. (2002). Clubs to Companies: Notes on the Decline of Political Culture in Speeded Up Creative Worlds. *Cultural Studies* 16(4): 516–31.

McRobbie, A. (2007). Top Girls? Young Women and the Post-feminist Sexual Contract. *Cultural Studies* 21(4–5): 718–37.

McRobbie, A. (2009). *The Aftermath of Feminism: Gender, Culture and Social Change*. London: Sage.

Marx, K. (1973). *Economic and Philosophic Manuscripts 1844*, Dirk J. Struik (ed); Martin Milligan (trans.). London: Lawrence & Wishart.

Mills, C. Wright (1951). *White Collar: The American Middle Classes*. New York: Oxford University Press.

Mitropoulos, A. (2006). "Precari-us?" *Mute Magazine*. January 9. <http://www.metamute.org/en/Precari-us>; accessed September 17, 2010.

Moran, J. (2005). *Reading the Everyday*. London: Routledge.

Morgenstern, J. (2001). *Time Management from the Inside Out: The Foolproof System for Taking Control of Your Schedule – and Your Life*. London: Hodder.

Morris, M. (1996). Crazy Talk is Not Enough. Guest Editorial. *Environment and Planning D: Society and Space* 1(14): 384–94.

Morris, M. (2009). Grizzling About Facebook. *Australian Humanities Review* 47 (November) <http://www.australianhumanitiesreview.org/

archive/Issue-November-2009/morris.html>; accessed September 27, 2010.

Morrison, L. (2007). Interview with Kiley Gaffney. *Pig City Then and Now: A Symposium on the Past, Present and Future of the Rock Music Industry in Brisbane.* University of Queensland. July 13.

Mosco, V. and McKercher, C. (2008). *The Laboring of Communication: Will Knowledge Workers of the World Unite?* Lanham, MD: Lexington Books.

Moses, A. (2009). Facebook Discipline May Be Illegal: Expert. *Sydney Morning Herald.* April 3. <http://www.smh.com.au/articles/2009/04/03/1238261779328.html>; accessed September 26, 2010.

Murphy, K. (2008). Work-anywhere Devices Tip Balance against Having a Life. *The Australian,* IT Defrag, July 22.

Neilson, B. (2009). The World Seen from a Taxi: Students-migrants-workers in the Global Multiplication of Labour. *Subjectivity* 29: 425–44.

Neilson, B. and Rossiter, N. (2008). Precarity as a Political Concept, or, Fordism as Exception. *Theory, Culture & Society* 25(7–8): 51–72.

Nicholas, P. (2010). Locate your Comfort Zone. *The Weekend Australian,* Weekend Professional, January 9–10.

Nippert-Eng, C. (1996). *Home and Work: Negotiating Boundaries Through Everyday Life.* Chicago, IL: University of Chicago Press.

Nippert-Eng, C. (2010). *Islands of Privacy.* Chicago, IL: University of Chicago Press.

Oakley, A. (1974). *The Sociology of Housework.* London: Martin Robertson. Reprinted with new Introduction. Oxford: Blackwell, 1985.

Oakley, K. (2004). Not So Cool Britannia: The Role of the Creative Industries in Economic Development. *International Journal of Cultural Studies* 7(1): 67–77.

O'Connor (2008). Want to Get Ahead? Sit Properly. *The Sydney Morning Herald,* My Career, April 18–19.

Osborne, L. (2009). Being Connected: Australians' Take-up and Use of Broadband. Presentation on behalf of Australian Communications and Media Authority to *Self, Place, and Broadband Connectivity: Making and Making Do* Workshop, University of Wollongong, February 12.

Ouellette, L. (forthcoming). Women's Work: Affective Labor and Convergence Culture. *Cultural Studies* Special Issue on Rethinking Convergence/Culture.

Pateman, C. (1988). *The Sexual Contract.* Stanford, CA: Stanford University Press.

Peters, T. (1998). The Brand Called You. *Fast Company,* 10 (August). Republished December 18, 2007. <http://www.fastcompany.com/magazine/10/brandyou.html>.

Potts, Jason D. and Cunningham, Stuart D. (2008). Four Models of the Creative Industries. *International Journal of Cultural Policy* 14(3): 233–47.

Pratt, A. C. (2009). Policy Transfer and the Field of the Cultural and Creative Industries: Learning from Europe? In Kong, L. and

O'Connor, J. (eds), *Creative Economies, Creative Cities: Asian–European Perspectives*. Heidelberg: Springer, pp. 9–23.

Putnam, R. (2000). *Bowling Alone: The Collapse and Revival of American Community*. New York: Simon & Schuster.

Qiu, J. (2009). *Working Class Network Society: Communication Technology and the Information Have-less in Urban China*. Cambridge, MA: MIT Press.

Qualman, E. (2009). *Socialnomics: How Social Media Transforms the Way We Live and Do Business*. New Jersey: Wiley & Sons.

Race, K. (forthcoming). Party Animals: The Significance of Drug Practices in the Materialization of Urban Gay Identity. In S. Fraser and D. Moore (eds), *Drugs, Health and Crime: Critical Perspectives*. Cambridge: Cambridge University Press.

Radway, Janice A. (1984). *Reading the Romance: Women, Patriarchy, and Popular Literature*. Chapel Hill, NC: University of North Carolina Press.

Robertson, J. (2010). Stephanie Rice Loses Sponsor Jaguar after Anti-gay Tweet. *The Courier-Mail*, September 7, 2010. <http://www.news.com. au/business/stephanie-rice-loses-sponsor-jaguar-after-anti-gay-tweet/ story-e6frfm1i-1225915098261>; accessed September 26, 2010.

Rogers, I. (2011, forthcoming). *Musicians and Aspiration: Exploring the Rock Dream in Independent Music*. PhD Thesis. University of Queensland.

Rose, N. (1999a). *Governing the Soul: The Shaping of the Private Self*. London: Free Association Books, 2nd edn.

Rose, N. (1999b). *Powers of Freedom: Reframing Political Thought*. Cambridge: Cambridge University Press.

Ross, A. (2003). *No-Collar: The Humane Workplace and its Hidden Costs*. New York: Basic Books.

Ross, A. (2004). The Mental Labor Problem. In *Low Pay: High Profile*. New York: The New Press, pp. 191–232.

Ross, A. (2006). *Fast Boat to China: Corporate Flight and the Consequences for Free Trade – Lessons from Shanghai*. New York: Pantheon.

Ross, A. (2008). The New Geography of Work: Power to the Precarious? *Theory, Culture & Society* 25(7–8): 31–49.

Ross, A. (2009). *Nice Work If You Can Get It: Life and Labor in Precarious Times*. New York: New York University Press.

Ryan, R. (2009). What I'm Working On: Isabel Metz. *Australian Financial Review Boss*. April: 53.

Sassen, S. (2006). *A Sociology of Globalization*. New York: W. W. Norton

Scott, M. (2010). Address to the National Press Club, February 11.

Sennett, R. (1998). *The Corrosion of Character: The Personal Consequences of Work in the New Capitalism*. New York: W. W. Norton.

Sennett, R. (2006). *The Culture of the New Capitalism*. New Haven, CT: Yale University Press.

Sherwell, P. (2010). Lots of Friends, So Many Enemies. telegraph.co.uk. <http://www.telegraph.co.uk/technology/facebook/8024056/Lots-of-friends-so-many-enemies.html>.

Shirky, C. (2008). *Here Comes Everybody: The Power of Organizing Without Organizations*. London: Penguin.

Solove, D. (2007). *The Future of Reputation: Gossip, Rumor, and Privacy on the Internet*. New Haven, CT: Yale University Press.

Stafford, A. (2006). *Pig City: From The Saints to Savage Garden*. St Lucia: University of Queensland Press. First published 2004.

Stirling, J. (2010). 'Sickies' Rise in GFC Aftermath. Weekend Professional, *The Weekend Australian*, May 15–16.

Streeter, T. (2003). The Romantic Self and the Politics of Internet Commercialization. *Cultural Studies* 17(5): 648–68.

Streeter, T. (2005). The Moment of Wired. *Critical Inquiry* 31 (summer): 755–79.

Streeter, T. (2010). *The Net Effect: Romanticism, Capitalism, and the Internet*. New York: New York University Press.

Sydney Morning Herald (2006). A Guide to Pocket Offices. *Icon*, June 3.

Sydney Morning Herald (2009). Ruthless Recruiting. Memo, My Career, May 30–31.

Taskin, L. and Devos, V. (2005). Paradoxes from the Individualization of Human Resource Management: The Case of Telework. *Journal of Business Ethics* 62: 13–24.

Taylor, J. (2000a). Queensland Woos Virgin. *The World Today*. ABC Radio. 3 February. <http://www.abc.net.au/worldtoday/stories/s97613.htm>; accessed September 20, 2010.

Taylor, J. (2000b). Queensland Revels in Virgin Win. PM. ABC Radio. 3 February. <http://www.abc.net.au/pm/stories/s97703.htm>; accessed September 20, 2010.

Terranova, T. (2004). *Network Culture: Politics for the Information Age*. London: Pluto Press.

Tracy, J. F. and Hayashi, M. L. (2007). A Libratariat? Labor, Technology, and Librarianship in the Information Age. In McKercher, C. and Mosco, V. (eds), *Knowledge Workers in the Information Society*. Plymouth: Lexington Books, pp. 53–67.

Tremblay, D-G., Paquet, R., and Najem, E. (2006). Telework: A Way to Balance Work and Family or an Increase in Work–Family Conflict? *Canadian Journal of Communication* 31: 715–31.

Trinca, H. and Fox, C. (2004). *Better than Sex: How a Whole Generation Got Hooked on Work*. Sydney: Random House.

Tsang, S. (2008). Soothe the Savage Inbox. *Sydney Morning Herald, The Guide*, October 13.

Turkle, Sherry (2011). *Alone Together: Why We Expert More from Technology and Less from Each Other*. New York: Basic Books.

Turner, G. (2010). *Ordinary People and the Media: The Demotic Turn*. London: Sage.

Turner, F. (2006). *From Counterculture to Cyberculture: Stewart Brand, the Whole Earth Network, and the Rise of Digital Utopianism*. Chicago, IL: University of Chicago Press.

Turner, F. (2009). Dreaming the End of Bureaucracy: Network Theory and the Legacy of the Counterculture. Presentation at *The Internet as Playground and Factory* conference, The New School, NYC, November.

Turner, K. (2009). Finding the Right "Brand Voice" on Twitter. *Mashable: The Social Media Guide*. March 9. <http://mashable.com/2009/03/09/twitter-brand-voice/>.

Vanni, A. I. and Tari, M. (2005). The Life and Deeds of San Precario, Patron Saint of Precarious Workers and Lives, *Fibreculture Journal* 5: 1–11.

Vascellaro, J. E. (2009). Twitter Works to Control Growth. *The Australian*, May 27, p. 32. Reprinted from the *Wall Street Journal*.

Virno, P. (1996). The Ambivalence of Disenchantment. In M. Hardt and P. Virno (eds), *Radical Thought in Italy: A Potential Politics*. Minneapolis, MN: University of Minnesota Press, pp. 1–10.

Ward, Susan and O'Regan, Tom (2007) Servicing "the other Hollywood": The Vicissitudes of an International Television Production Location. *International Journal of Cultural Studies* 10(2): 167–85.

Weber, M. (1976). *The Protestant Ethic and the Spirit of Capitalism*. London: George Allen & Unwin, 2nd edn. First published 1930.

Willis, P. E. (1977). *Learning to Labour: How Working Class Kids Get Working Class Jobs*. Westmead: Saxon House.

Whyte, W. (1963). *The Organization Man*. Harmondsworth: Penguin. Originally published 1956.

Wilson, J. (2007). "Digital White Flight"? Facebook, Class and Social Networking. *New Media Research Group Blog*, <http://spooner.beds.ac.uk/nmrg/?p=60>; accessed 23/3/10.

Wilson, N. H. and Lande, B. J. (2005). Feeling Capitalism: A Conversation with Arlie Hochschild. *Journal of Consumer Culture* 5(3): 275–88

Woolf, V. (1929). *A Room of One's Own*. London: Hogarth Press.

Wynhausen, E. (2005). *Dirt Cheap: Life at the Wrong End of the Job Market*. Sydney: Pan Macmillan.

Zuboff, S. (1988). *In the Age of the Smart Machine: The Future of Work and Power*. New York: Basic Books.

Zylinska, J. (2009). *Bioethics in the Age of New Media*. Cambridge, MA: MIT Press.

Index